AN ESSAY

ON THE

HISTORY AND MANAGEMENT

OF

LITERARY, SCIENTIFIC, & MECHANICS' INSTITUTIONS

and Especially
How far they may be Developed and Combined
so as to promote
THE MORAL WELL BEING AND INDUSTRY OF
THE COUNTRY

BY

JAMES HOLE

with a new index

Routledge
Taylor & Francis Group
LONDON AND NEW YORK

First published 1853 by Frank Cass and Company Limited

2 Park Square, Milton Park, Abingdon, Oxon OX14 4RN
711 Third Avenue, New York, NY 10017, USA

Routledge is an imprint of the Taylor & Francis Group, an informa business

First issued in paperback 2016

New impression 1970

Transferred to Digital Printing 2006

ISBN 978-0-7146-2410-5 (hbk)
ISBN 978-1-138-99351-8 (pbk)

Publisher's Note
The publisher has gone to great lengths to ensure the quality of this reprint but points out that some imperfections in the original may be apparent

THE SOCIAL HISTORY OF SCIENCE

No. 5

General Editor: Dr. ROY M. MACLEOD
Reader in History and Social Studies of Science
at the University of Sussex

AN ESSAY

ON THE

HISTORY AND MANAGEMENT

OF

LITERARY, SCIENTIFIC, & MECHANICS' INSTITUTIONS

AN ESSAY

ON THE

HISTORY AND MANAGEMENT

OF

LITERARY, SCIENTIFIC, & MECHANICS' INSTITUTIONS;

AND ESPECIALLY

HOW FAR THEY MAY BE DEVELOPED AND COMBINED,

SO AS TO PROMOTE

THE MORAL WELL-BEING AND INDUSTRY OF THE COUNTRY.

BY JAMES HOLE, ESQ.,

HONORARY SECRETARY OF THE YORKSHIRE UNION OF MECHANICS' INSTITUTIONS.

"Nemo Labori Musas vetet."

PUBLISHED UNDER THE SANCTION OF THE SOCIETY OF ARTS.

LONDON:

LONGMAN, BROWN, GREEN, AND LONGMANS.

1853.

Train up thy children, England,
In the ways of righteousness, and feed them
With the bread of wholesome doctrine.
Where hast thou thy mines — but in their industry?
Thy bulwarks where — but in their breasts?

SOUTHEY.

L'éducation est l'avenir des peuples.

ADVERTISEMENT.

The Society for the Encouragement of Arts, Manufactures, and Commerce, in their Prize List for the Session 1852–3, offered the Society's Medal and a Premium of £50 for the best Essay on the History and Management of Literary, Scientific, and Mechanics' Institutions; and especially how far, and in what manner, they may be developed and combined, so as to promote the moral well-being and industry of the country. In consequence of this announcement a number of Essays were received; and, on the request of the judges to whom they were referred, the prize was awarded to the Essay with the motto "Nemo Labori Musas vetet," sent in by Mr. James Hole, of Leeds. It was a part of the conditions under which the prize was offered, that the successful candidate should publish his essay, under the sanction of the Society.

CONTENTS.

CHAPTER I.

CHAP. II.

APPENDICES.

MECHANICS' INSTITUTES.

CHAPTER I.

HISTORY.

THE year 1851 will ever be memorable as the epoch of the Great Exhibition. We then witnessed, collected into one focus, the best results of the skill, taste, and industry of the world. Different nations, no longer rivalling each other in military contests or diplomatic chicane, tried whether peace could not show more glorious victories than war! Each learnt by comparison its peculiar merits or special deficiencies, and every member of that Congress of Nations was benefited by the lesson.

Of the many consequences flowing from this grand organisation of the products of industry, we note the steady rise of a feeling for the industrial education of the people in the minds of those whose interest in the Exhibition was not confined to the temporary amusement of a few hours. If so much had been done *without* any special culture on the part of the people, how much more might be done *with* it? If we beheld the labours of our superior workmen only, developed by the energy of the capitalists, what might be anticipated when *all* our people should have received the benefits of instruction? Moreover, with such wonders of skill and ingenuity before us, applied to everything that could minister to human need, surely the knowledge that enabled us to achieve all this was of some importance, and ought to meet with befitting treatment at our hands. As mere knowledge, it was as dignified as the lore taught in our Colleges and Universities, and in its direct influence on human happiness the two could not for one moment be compared.

With a surplus in hand of 150,000*l.*, for which, amidst many claimants, there were none whose proposals would have satisfied the nation, it was wisely determined to provide "a common centre of action for the dissemination of a knowledge of science and art among all classes," to increase the means of industrial education, and extend the influence of science and art upon productive industry; and although the surplus was to be applied in "furtherance of *one* large institution, devoted to the purpose of instruction, adequate for the extended wants of industry," yet it is to be "in connexion with similar institutions in the provinces."

The Commissioners, we think, acted wisely in preferring to secure one comprehensive Institute in London, rather than distributing the fund in driblets among local Institutes, where the result would have been comparatively small, or at least less visible or encouraging. It would be a great mistake, however, to imagine that the erection of one temple to art, science, and industrial education in the metropolis, however magnificent as a whole, and however complete in all its details, will satisfy the wants of the country. London is not Great Britain; and though the centre of the largest population, it is not the chief centre of those industries which make Great Britain the workshop of the world. Manchester and its surrounding towns, Stockport, Bolton, Preston and Blackburn, Birmingham, the Potteries, Nottingham, Leicester, Leeds and Newcastle, Bradford,

Sheffield, Huddersfield, and Halifax;—one has but to name these densely-populated centres of the productive power of the nation, to see that any scheme for the diffusion of the arts and sciences whose operation should be confined to London, would fail in its most important function. Indeed, all the requisitions to the Commissioners from the provincial towns insist upon local establishments in connexion with the Metropolitan Institute, as a part of the scheme.[1]

Neglect of the interests of science and art in this country on the part of the nation, is a complaint so often repeated as to be almost stale. Much has been done by individuals and voluntary associations, but done without system and without relation to actual wants, so that a large amount of effort has been unproductive. An unreasonable jealousy of all interference of Government on the part of the people, and an almost utter indifference on the part of the Government itself to its own highest duties, have in past years prevailed. The intense worship of wealth and rank compared with that paid to intellect, and the struggle of parties and factions on great political questions, have also contributed to this neglect. While other countries have been moving unostentatiously onward in the path of education, both for youths and adults, and have, without a tithe of our natural advantages, become able to tread closely on our heels in the march of civilisation, this nation has been indulging its characteristic self-complacency, and looking with supremest contempt on "those foreigners." With frigid indifference we have seen growing up amid our refined and luxurious civilisation, the densest, brutalest ignorance,—side by side with our enormous wealth, an incredible amount of human misery,—the palaces of the rich elbowed by the nests of fever and the hovels of despairing wretchedness. While we have

[1] See Appendix A.

been squabbling about who shall teach the children, and what they shall be taught, hundreds of thousands have grown up untaught in all save vice. And now that the Great Exhibition is over, we learn that even the shop is in danger,—a fact, we may hope, that will leave its due impression. More remarkable than even these contrasts is the noise we make when we are about to extend some small help to education. "Speech from the throne," "Strong feeling in the country," "Decided expression of the House," "Editorial thunder in all newspapers,"—and all for a few thousands; while a million or two more or less, in Army or Navy estimates, would not have created a tithe of the excitement. And yet what item is there in the Chancellor of the Exchequer's budget which can rank for one moment with that devoted to advance the intelligence of the country? What "interests," West Indian, Cotton, Shipping, or any other, can be compared with the "Working-Class Interest," and what duties of more moment than attention to the moral and social advancement of our swarming population?

What part government should take in promoting adult instruction, is a question of expediency and of public opinion. It must, like all questions of government interference, be decided upon its own merits; and we shall offer in the course of this paper some remarks bearing upon it. The country is indebted to the Society of Arts for mooting the question, How are Scientific, Literary, and Mechanics' Institutes to be improved? For this opens up the whole question of adult instruction. In promoting the Great Exhibition, the Society of Arts rendered the state some service; to their lectures we are probably indebted for the magnificent scheme proposed by the Royal Commissioners. But the Society of Arts will confer a boon on the country greater than either the Exhibition or the Industrial University, if it can increase the utility of our Mechanics' Institutes, and diffuse their advantages among large numbers of our people. Its exertion in calling the great meeting of delegates from these Institutes on the 18th May, 1852, proves that it has a single-minded desire to secure this end; and if success wait on this endeavour, that day will be a memorable one. To ascertain the nature and character of these Institutes, what are their defects and advantages, and, above all, how they can be improved and their powers of good developed, will materially contribute to that great object.

The history of Mechanics' Institutes has usually been dated from the 2d of December, 1823, when the London Mechanics' Institution was formally established. Some controversy has existed as to who first founded these Institutes. The highest merit seems rather for first making them known and appreciated, than for any actual discovery, since voluntary isolated associations of the kind existed prior to the above date. With the London Mechanics' Institute originated a movement of the most important kind, which gave a clearly defined purpose and shape to wants that the progress of civilisation had created. That which has been said of the art of printing is true of the Mechanics' Institute, viz. that if it had not been discovered in the way it was, the time had come when it must have been discovered, for it had become a necessity of the age. A self-governing machinery for the purpose of diffusing knowledge among the labouring classes, could have no existence when arts, sciences, and literature were regarded as the refined luxury of a few—when the labourer was considered simply as a superior sort of cattle grown for the behoof of his master, endued with no higher qualities than strength and obedience, and whom cultivation would not only unfit for his station, but render less happy. We are far from thinking such notions extinct—*we know they are not;* but they survive only in those nooks where the belief in witchcraft, and other absurdities of our forefathers, still linger, and in another generation the schoolmaster will have chased them utterly away.

There is little doubt that the general establishment of Sunday Schools did very much to prepare the way for the establishment of Mechanics' Institutes. Reading and writing were taught to the children in them, with which evening classes were afterwards connected for the instruction of adults. In 1789 a society was established in Birmingham for instructing young men. Writing, book-keeping, arithmetic, geography, and drawing were taught, lectures were delivered, a library was formed; in fact, the "Sunday Society," or, as it was afterwards entitled, the "Birmingham Brotherly Society," resembled in most respects a large number of Mechanics' Institutes of the present day. In 1796, Anderson's University was incorporated by the magistrates and council of Glasgow. Dr. John Anderson bequeathed the larger portion of his property for "the improvement of human nature, of science, and of his country." The University was to consist of four colleges besides a school. The four colleges were for the arts, medicine, law, and theology. The subjects taught, and the other arrangements, sufficiently show that the Institution was not contemplated for the operative classes, but for those in the middle rank. Fortunately for the former, in three years after the establishment of the university (1799), Dr. George Birkbeck was appointed the professor of natural philosophy. He required apparatus for his lectures, and the Glasgow of that time (not one-fifth of the present Glasgow) could not furnish it without a resort to the workshops, and this brought him in contact with the mechanics and artizans. He perceived their deficiency in scientific information; he learnt their wish to remedy this want, and resolved to supply them with the means. Why, said he, are these minds left without the means of obtaining that knowledge they so ardently desire? Why are the avenues to science barred against them, because they are poor? He resolved to offer them a gratuitous course of elementary philosophical lectures. To treat his proposal as "visionary" and "absurd," was but to repeat the welcome which the would-be wise have bestowed on every improvement since the world began. They predicted "that if invited, the mechanics would not come; that if they did come, they would not listen; and if they did listen, they would not comprehend."[1]

Sizzi the astronomer assailed the discovery of Jupiter's satellites by Galileo in the same style. "The satellites are invisible to the naked eye, and therefore can exercise no influence over the earth, and therefore would be useless, and therefore do not exist." Birkbeck, like Galileo, chose to believe his own, rather than any secondary testimony. The offer was made to them, — "they came, they listened, and conquered, — conquered the prejudice that would have consigned them to the dominion of interminable ignorance." Dr. Birkbeck conducted his "mechanics" class for four years. On his removal to London in 1804, Dr. Ure, his successor, carried it on with equal zeal and success, and in 1808 added a library. For a few years it continued; then it declined, owing to the neglect of the managers of the University; then was revived; and ultimately seceded altogether in 1823, and formed the Glasgow Mechanics' Institute, five months previous to the formation of the London Mechanics' Institute. In the same month was established the Liverpool Mechanics' and Apprentices' Library. Previous, however, to either of these institutions being established, there had been formed, in April, 1821, the Edinburgh School of Arts (now the Watt Institution) by Mr. Leonard Horner. Of this Institution we shall have to say more hereafter, as it is one of the very few Institutes in the kingdom which, *so far as the*

[1] Dr. Birkbeck's address at the London Mechanics' Institute.

plan of instruction is concerned, is worthy of imitation. It was not, however, till the establishment of the London Mechanics' Institute, that the subject began to attract general attention. In 1814 Mr. F. Dick wrote five papers in the Monthly Magazine on the formation of Literary and Philosophical Societies for the humbler classes, containing many valuable suggestions. His proposals seem to have scarcely attracted any notice. In 1817 an Institution entitled the Mechanical Institution was established in London; but neither this, nor the Glasgow, the Liverpool, or the Haddington Institutes, all of which were established in the same year, and previous to the London Mechanics' Institute, awakened public attention to the subject, any more than the labours of Dr. Birkbeck in Glasgow twenty-three years previously had done. To him is undoubtedly due the honour of having originated the system of offering scientific instruction in an accessible form to the working classes. But the honour of establishing the London Mechanics' Institute twenty-three years later, and which gave the first impulse to the subject throughout the provinces, must be shared by the editors of the Mechanics' Magazine, Messrs. Robertson and Hodgskin, especially the former, who proposed it in an article on the subject in the number for October 11th, 1823. Dr. Birkbeck, on its proposal, immediately took an active part in promoting it. Henry Brougham advocated it, and, in an article on the scientific education of the people in the Edinburgh Review of October, 1824, signed William Davis, gave the subject publicity, and stimulated to the formation of many of the provincial Institutes. The proprietor of the Morning Chronicle and Observer newspapers put down his name for one hundred and twenty guineas; and altogether it received donations in money to the amount of above a thousand pounds in the first year of its existence. At its second anniversary, the Duke of Sussex presided, around whom were clustered many of the active men of the day,—Brougham, Denman, Hobhouse, Lushington, Birkbeck, and other less known personages, that the lapse of a generation has consigned to oblivion. A large building was purchased at a cost of 4000*l.*, of which 3700*l.* was advanced by Dr. Birkbeck, and two-thirds of this sum remains unpaid to this day. For this munificent aid, which had an effect on the formation of Mechanics' Institutions analogous to that which the Liverpool and Manchester Railway has had upon railway locomotion,—for this truly national service, the government had the generosity the other day to offer 50*l.* per annum to Dr. Birkbeck's widow, an offer which was *declined.*

The publicity given to the nature and objects of these Institutions by the auspicious commencement of the London Mechanics' Institution, speedily led to their establishment in the principal towns. In 1824, Institutions were established in Aberdeen, Dundee, Leeds, Newcastle on Tyne, Alnwick, Dunbar, and Lancaster; and in 1825, in Manchester, Birmingham, Norwich, Devonport, Plymouth, Portsmouth, Ashton, Bolton, Hexham, Ipswich, Lewes, Louth, Shrewsbury, Halifax, Hull, and other places.[1]

The present year will witness the thirtieth anniversary of the establishment of the London Mechanics' Institute. In that period Institutes of the same nature, but established under various names, as Mechanics' Institutes, Literary Societies, Mutual Improvement Societies, have increased to the number of 700, containing 120,000 members, thus classified[2]:

[1] For full information on the subject, we refer the reader to the History of "*Adult Education,* by Dr. J. W. Hudson," the completest work on the subject. Consult also the Manual for Mechanics' Institutes, published under the superintendence of the Society for the Diffusion of Useful Knowledge, which has lost little of its value by the lapse of fourteen years.

[2] History of Adult Education, p. 6.

	Number of Institutes.	Members.	Volumes.	Issues of Books, 1850.	Number of Persons attending Evening Classes.	Number of Lectures delivered in 1850.	News Rooms.
England	610	102,050	691,500	1,820,748	16,020	5,034	372
Wales	12	1,472	6,855	16,800	280	115	8
Scotland	55	12,554	59,661	154,747	1,638	481	15
Ireland	25	4,005	57,500	33,800	182	210	13
Total	702	120,081	815,516	2,026,095	18,120	5,840	408

This summary does not, probably, contain the whole number, and is certainly rather under than over the truth.

It would be difficult to estimate too highly the amount of good which this vast machinery has effected. We have not indeed, in these prosaic figures, the record of any great event,—of one of those deeds which strike men dumb with admiration or amazement. There is nothing to attract the novelist to weave around it the ornaments of his fancy,—little perhaps to tempt the historian to linger on the record; yet how trivial, in relation to human weal, are many of their themes compared with this! Mechanics' Institutes have become an element of English life—a power acting and reacting for good on thousands and tens of thousands of our population, and, through them, on yet unborn generations. History, when rightly written, will give a larger place to the exertions of Brougham and Birkbeck, than to the greatest success of our greatest warrior. This will at last become but a date; while a true and great principle, despised when first inaugurated, grows like the stately oak with slow growth, but finally gives shelter and repose to the nations. The founders of Mechanics' Institutes pronounced with authority that the labouring man was destined to be a rational agent, and that his nature was "sinned against" when, from any cause, his mental powers were suppressed. They said for him, "The owner of this poor pair of hands, working for daily bread, is something other than the horse, which, having done its day's toil, is content with its feed of corn and share of sleep. To these hands there belongs a human head, with all its powers and passions, its wants and sympathies! Shall they be extinguished, —go down to death and 'give no sign'—useless to himself, and evil to others? or shall he too become a thinking, intelligent being, and his life have a pregnant meaning for himself and his fellows? This is the alternative:—

> 'For 'tis his nature to advance or die;
> He stands not still, but or decays or grows
> Into a boundless blessing, which may vie
> With the immortal lights in their eternity.'"

Whatever we may think of Mechanics' Institutes as educational establishments, they have certainly, and perhaps more than any other agency, helped to form a sound public opinion as to the necessity and duty of popular education. At their lectures and social meetings this has ever been, directly or indirectly, the noble theme. They have established the right of the people to culture—more primary and pressing than the right to labour or the Franchise; a right great as the right to live, since it makes life worth living for. The large circulation of their books has cultivated a taste for reading, and rendered it profitable to produce the most excellent works at an almost nominal price. Some people are disposed to regard the cheapness of books as the cause of the great increase of reading: it would be truer to say, that primarily it was rather the effect of the increased taste for reading, which these Institutions first helped to foster. They created a paying public to take them. Many of the books are read by the family of the member as well as by himself. When a man has acquired a taste for reading, he will not be content with the books of the library. It was Mechanics' Institutions which created a popular taste for good music. Cheap concerts originated with the Mechanics' Institution at Manchester. Crude as is the knowledge conveyed by Institutional lectures, there is no doubt that they have facilitated the progress of social and sanitary reform. People have got to know a little about ventilation, about draining, about smoke consuming, and other practical matters. Though politics are excluded, newspapers are not; and a superior class newspaper has come within the reach of the people. The tone of thought on many political topics has become elevated. Newspapers of both sides are admitted: people get to see both sides of a question; partizanship is diminished; honesty and ability are found not to be the exclusive property of one side, and stupidity and villany of the other. This very valuable result has been strengthened by the bringing of all sorts of men together at their social meetings. We have seen the successful and rejected candidates meet, the day after an election, on such an occasion, and forget all the animosity of party in the common desire to elevate their fellow men.

Though, in the lapse of thirty years since the London Mechanics' Institute first gave the impetus to these Institutions, much has been done for education, much more yet waits to be accomplished. It was the glaring disparity that existed between the vast progress which had been achieved in this country in material wealth, and the low moral and intellectual state of those whose toil chiefly produced it, that struck the friends of education a generation ago. Looking now at the growth of the cotton, silk, woollen, iron, and other trades and manufactures, the increased powers of machinery and of locomotion,—in short, the additions to the national wealth in every department, it is impossible not to feel that the rapid material progress of the nation has not been accompanied by a proportional moral and intellectual advancement of the artizan class.

The reasons which then prompted the friends of popular enlightenment to urge the establishment of mechanics' Institutions, are not less valid now. Happily, the means to effect social improvements, and the experience to conduct them, are far greater now than they were at that time. The present is a period highly favourable for such efforts. No question of great political moment agitates the country. The emigration to Australia, and the cheapness of food, have combined to raise the working classes to a position of comparative comfort; and should the thunder-clouds of war happily pass by, and the stream of emigration continue unchecked, the means of comfort and material happiness will be still further augmented. But should it unfortunately happen that unforeseen disasters overtake our country, and the present smiling prospect become overclouded, should one of those trade-storms, in past years of such frequent recurrence, again sweep over us, it would be found that very little had been done either by or for the working classes to remove the intense evils of such times. The same unmeaning agitations for political changes as a panacea for social evils, — the same ill-feeling between capital and labour, — and the same reckless improvidence, — would be nearly as marked and manifest as before. Notwithstanding the present constant employment, with wages above the average, should trade come to a temporary lull, thousands of operatives would in the second week have to pledge their garments and goods; while a month's want of work would suffice to render them claimants for parish pay.

As History is philosophy teaching by *example*, so all attempts to improve Mechanics' Institutes, whether by enlarging the scope of their objects or extending their influence over the population, must be based upon a knowledge of their history and character. What were their objects when first established? How far have their proposed ends been attained? And if they have failed, for what reason? These are questions which must precede any effectual plans for future improvements.

One of the most clearly defined and primary aims of the first founders of Mechanics' Institutes,—with some of the promoters almost the exclusive aim,—was to impart instruction to workmen in those rules and principles which lie at the basis of the arts they practise. Learning a trade meant, as it still means, a training of the hands to perform certain operations with tolerable dexterity, while the head of the workman is little if at all engaged therein. The *reason* of the thing, the why and wherefore the act should be performed in a certain way and in no other, is too often regarded by the workman rather as the business of the master or the foreman than his own. "Why should he bother his head when he doesn't get paid for it?"—intellectual labour being as much looked upon as a task as if you asked him to work overhours without extra wages. It is obvious that the artist who paints without any knowledge of the principles and harmony of colours, or the bleacher, dyer, or calico printer who knows nothing of chemistry, must work from mere imitation. The man working without any knowledge of the laws whereby the result is achieved, is like a machine, moving as he is moved; or his mind resembles the instinct of the bee and the beaver, which never improves. Such a one can never feel the same pleasure in his employment as he whose intellect is in his work. If fashion, accident, or improvement requires changes in the process, the ignorant workman finds the greatest difficulty in accommodating himself to the new plan, and is the most doggedly obstinate in resisting its introduction. He is the least likely to hit upon any invention or discovery to facilitate his labour; and should accident put him on the track, he cannot follow it for want of the needful light to guide him. And if, as often happens, machinery renders his employment quite useless, he has neither energy nor intelligence enough to take up with the new plan, nor to throw himself into any other branch of industry, should such be open to him.

Such were the reasons which struck Dr. Birkbeck half a century ago, when professor of natural philosophy at Anderson's University in Glasgow, and that made him take his first steps for the removal of the evils perceived. "I have become convinced," says he, "that much pleasure would be communicated to the mechanic in the exercise of his art, and that the mental vacancy which follows a cessation from bodily toil would often be agreeably occupied by a few systematic philosophical ideas, upon which, at his leisure, he might meditate. It must be acknowledged, too, that greater satisfaction in the execution of machinery must be experienced, when the uses to which it may be applied, and the principles on which it operates, are well understood, than where the manual part alone is known, the artist remaining entirely ignorant of everything besides; indeed, I have lately had frequent opportunities of observing with how much additional alacrity a piece of work has been undertaken when the circumstances were such as I have now stated." His first attempt, about the year 1800, was the delivery of a course of lectures on the "Mechanical Affections of solid and fluid Bodies," "solely for Persons engaged in the Mechanical Arts."

The first report of the Edinburgh School of Arts was of the same tendency, and this society was almost the only one that has continued to adhere to its first objects. It was formed, says the report, for affording "instruction in the various branches of science which are of practical application to mechanics in their several trades, so that they may the better comprehend the reason for each individual operation that passes through their hands, and have more certain rules to follow than the mere imitation of what they may have seen done by another. It is not intended to teach the trade of the carpenter, the mason, the dyer, or any other particular business; but there is no trade which does not depend, more or less, upon scientific principles; and to teach what these are, and to point out their practical application, will form the business of this establishment."

In all these Institutes the main feature of the programme of operations was the scientific education of the people by means of lectures, classes, and books on scientific subjects. In the School of Arts the lectures were strictly of this character, and *no book was admitted into the library but what related to science or art.*

The preamble of the Manchester Mechanics' Institute, which has the honour of having erected the first building specially adapted for that object, was equally clear and explicit. After explaining the purposes enumerated above, it goes on to point out the means by which these were to be effected; namely, "by the delivery of lectures on the various sciences, and their practical application to the arts. Of these lectures, mechanical philosophy and chemistry will, of course, be leading subjects; and when their general principles, and those of other important sciences, have been made known, more minute and detailed instruction upon particular branches of art will form the subjects of subsequent lectures. It is intended that a suitable library shall be formed for circulation and reference, and that there shall be a collection of models, instruments, together with an experimental workshop and laboratory. It is hoped, also, that instruction may be given in the elements of geometry, in the higher branches of arithmetic, and in mechanical and architectural drawing."

That these intentions, on the part of the founders, have failed to be carried out in the large majority of

Institutes, is universally known. Mechanics' Institutes have failed,

1st. To attract the mechanic class (using the term in its generic sense, as including all classes of operatives).

2nd. To impart scientific instruction.

A few remarks on both these points will be needful.

We are far from considering the fact, that the benefits of Mechanics' Institutes have been derived by a class for whom they were not originally contemplated, as a matter of regret. It shows simply that another large class needed their advantages, and were more prepared to meet them. They did not deprive the working man of anything. If clerks and shopkeepers had not joined the Institutes, the operative would have no more participated in their benefits than he does now, perhaps much less, since, in many cases, there would have been no such place open to him at all. It shows that there were difficulties in the way of realising the objects proposed by the founders of Mechanics' Institutes which they had not contemplated. Assuming, however, for the moment, that all the members of these Institutes belonged to the class for whose benefit they were established, the numbers, as compared with the population, is perfectly insignificant. In Yorkshire, a district which contains the largest number of Institutes in proportion to the population of any in the kingdom, the number of members of Mechanics' Institutes will not form 2 per cent of the population. But, in reality, the Mechanics' Institutions belong to Mechanics only in name. In the Manchester Mechanics' Institutes (and in no Institute was the object of reaching the Mechanic class more sedulously kept in view) an analysis of the occupations of the members gives the following result on an average for seven years (1835 to 1841)[5]:—

[5] History of Adult Education, p. 131.

Merchants, Manufacturers, Artists, Architects, Engravers, Professional Men, Schoolmasters, and persons of no profession -	328
Clerks, Warehousemen, Shopkeepers, and their assistants - -	374
Mechanics, Millwrights, Overlookers, Spinners and Mill-hands, Building trades and other handicrafts - - - -	309
Ladies - - - - - - - - -	20
Youths - - - - - - - -	153
Total members -	1,184

The largest Institution of the kingdom in point of members is that of Leeds, yet the proportion of members to population is not above 1 in 50. The Leeds Institution (one of the best managed Institutions in the country) contains 2,166, who are thus classified:—

1st. Day-school Pupils - - - - - - -	211
2nd. Ladies - - - - - - - -	392
3rd. Persons paying 15*s*. per annum, and Life Members - -	687
4th. Persons receiving weekly wages, or Apprentices, paying 12*s*. per annum - - - - - - - -	503
5th. Persons under 18 years of age, paying 8*s*. per annum -	299
6th. Elementary class, paying 6*d*. per fortnight - - -	74
Total -	2,166

If we assume that the 4th, 5th, and 6th classes constitute the operative class of the Institution, but 876, or 1 in 115 of the population of the borough of Leeds belonging to the working classes, have embraced the advantages of the Institution. The total number of persons in the classes is 224, which represents more than the actual numbers because some pupils will be enrolled in more than one class. In the adjoining township of Hunslet, containing 20,000 inhabitants, principally operatives, the Institution, after lingering some time, is on the point of being closed for want of support. To take Huddersfield — the best example in the country of a Mechanics' Institute giving systematic instruction to the working classes, — the number of members is not 1 in 45 of the population. We cite these instances, not because the facts are special or exceptional, but because they fairly enough represent the state of the case as it exists in most of the large seats of population.[6]

A year after the establishment of the London Mechanics' Institution, we find the "Mechanics' Magazine" using language that might be used to-day: "What," it asks, "is three or four, or even seven hundred, compared with the number of mechanics in the metropolis? It is ridiculous to call this a representation of the working classes of London. One or two only of our large manufactories might have turned out the whole number." Mr. Hogg says, "From returns supplied by thirty-two of the principal Institutes in Lancashire and Cheshire, it is found that in only four do the working classes attend in considerable numbers, and these four are established in mere villages. Out of twenty-one Institutes in the Midland Counties, only three contained the working classes in considerable numbers."

The result is the more striking, because in such places the class who need that instruction which these Institutes were from the first intended to supply, is most numerous, and because no other means of obtaining it are in existence. Notwithstanding all that has been said on the subject of education, we are as yet but at the very threshold of any practical attempts to reach working men. In the smaller towns, several Institutes are composed chiefly of youths, with a sprinkling of working men, who join them, rather because, like some of the middle classes, they approve of the object, than from any direct educational advantages afforded to themselves. Out of 11,150 males, comprised in seventy-four Institutes, in Yorkshire, 2,908 (more than a fourth) were under eighteen, and of

6 It would only be necessary to give the amount of population and the numbers in the Institute of each place to prove this, but the fact is so well known as not to require it.

1,222 females in the same Institutes, 655 were below that age.[7]

The special causes of this state of things, so far as they depend on the character of the Institutes themselves, we shall hereafter discuss, but *one great and general cause* (which must have operated with fatal influence upon Mechanics' Institutes, however efficiently conducted), is the deficiency of elementary training for children. The adult has to commence that process in the Institution, which ought to have been completed before he entered its walls, and the time which he should be spending in the temple of knowledge, is taken up in mastering the keys of its portals. He commences when the character is formed, and above all when it is most difficult to induce habits of study.

The serious obstruction which it offers to the progress of Adult Instruction, and especially of any advanced kind of instruction, none but those who have laboured in this movement can form any adequate conception of. So long ago as 1840, the Central Committee of the Yorkshire Union of Mechanics' Institutes, deploring the non-success of the efforts to extend Mechanics' Institutes, thus speak in their Report:—

"The remote cause of this state of things, in the opinion of your Committee (and the conviction is daily becoming strengthened as their observation is extended), is unquestionably to be found in the absence of an early and sound intellectual and moral training for the mass of our operative population. Recent inquiries, conducted by various Statistical Societies, have demonstrated alike the bad quality and the insufficient amount of the education (if it may so be called) which is provided for a part of our infant and juvenile population; and have but too clearly shown that, with the exception of Sabbath School instruction, a large proportion receive

[7] Yorkshire Union Report, 1852.

no education whatever. What is taught fails to originate and strengthen a taste for reading, or a desire for the attainment of general knowledge; and hence it happens, that all the attractions of our Mechanics' Institutes, and all the substantial advantages offered at a cheap rate in their classes, fail to induce the great bulk of our juvenile operatives to enter them. They have neither the taste for the one, nor the right appreciation of the other. The Committee need not go far for the proof of this assertion, — it lies on the very surface of the Reports of the Union — namely, the vast disparity betwixt the total number of persons enrolled in the Institutes of the West Riding, and the total number of persons of the ages, and belonging to the class for which Mechanics' Institutes are provided, and in the fact, now universally acknowledged, that the members of Mechanics' Institutes are, nineteen-twentieths of them, not of the class of mechanics, but are connected with the higher branches of handicraft trades, or are clerks in offices, and, in many instances, young men connected with liberal professions." (Report, 1840.)

And again in the following year: —

"Amongst the opposing forces just alluded to, your Committee last year noticed the general apathy and indifference to knowledge amongst the operative classes, arising from the neglect of early elementary training, intellectual and moral. Again are they compelled to advert to the subject. They feel that the want of such training is a most serious and fatal evil, — a want, not merely productive of social inconvenience and derangement, but one which threatens, as its ultimate consequences, positive and absolute ruin. As society is now constituted, and looking to the kind of information diffused amongst the mass of the people, a sound intellectual and moral culture has become indispensable, not alone to the order, peace, and happiness of society, but to its very being. Without this culture, Mechanics' Institutes will never realise their original design."[8]

It has been said, that the mass of the working classes can never be expected to take great interest in intellectual pursuits,—that though you offer them fountains of living water you cannot persuade them to drink. Now, were this true, it would but show that it is doubly desirable to extend the means of instruction to the utmost, so that no chances of its reception should be lost. If but few seeds are destined to ripen into fruit, how much should we take care that none of those few be lost! But we deny the truth of the assertion altogether. Every extension of the means of instruction has largely increased the number of those availing themselves of it. The full capacity of the people has never yet been tried. Prior to the present generation, works on Education always meant the education of the gentleman, or the man raised by position above the necessity of labour. And even the term itself meant but the acquisition of the dead languages, and certain accomplishments. We are now learning to think that *all* may get at least some education, and by that term we are beginning to understand something more than the knowledge of words which have ceased to be spoken many centuries ago. Until the mind of the people has been properly trained, it is absurd to deduce from their apathy a natural antagonism to their intellectual culture. In those portions of the United States where most has been done for the instruction of the juvenile population, adult education has assumed an importance that we shall not speedily reach. Let us turn for a moment from the mortifying confession of what we have not done, to what our American relations have done. At the second quarterly meeting of the London Mechanics' Institute, June 2nd, 1824, a letter

[8] Yorkshire Union Report of years 1840 and 1841.

was read to the members from the secretary of the Franklin Institute for the State of Pennsylvania, announcing the formation of that society for carrying out similar objects to those of the London Mechanics' Institute. The Franklin Institute did not commence with half the number of members which the London Institute did, but very soon after the establishment "a regular system of lectures was at once adopted; four professorships created, namely, Natural Philosophy, Chemistry and Mineralogy, Architecture, and Mechanics; one evening, weekly, was set apart for lectures on miscellaneous subjects. A library, a mineralogical collection, a museum, and a cabinet of models commenced. An exhibition of manufactures was held, at which premiums were awarded." Compare its state now, after the lapse of an equal period, with the London Mechanics' Institute or any other in Great Britain. "Its library," says Dr. Hudson, "has grown to thirty-six thousand volumes. Its lectures are weekly, and free; its museum is perfect in the works of nature and art; it has a board of civil engineers belonging to it, who are bound to examine any machine or composition of matter that may be brought before them, and their report is published in the Monthly Journal of the Society. Annual fairs or exhibitions of the mechanical arts are also held." The Maryland Institute in Baltimore possesses all the features that distinguish the Franklin Institution, with the addition of its machine-shop for the accommodation of inventors, its laboratory for chemical experiments, its monthly journal, and its weekly mechanical and scientific newspapers."[9] Sir Charles Lyell, in his "Travels in North America," bears repeated testimony to facts of a similar character. For his own lectures (twelve on Geology), at the Lowell Institution, Boston, 4,500 tickets were bespoke

[9] History of Adult Education, p. 217.

some weeks before, and the class usually attending consisted of more than 3000 persons, whom it was necessary to divide into two sets, repeating to one of them, the next afternoon, the lecture delivered on the preceding evening.[10] At one small New England town he meets with a carpenter, who at the termination of his day's work is willing to pay a shilling to hear a lecture on the Astronomy of the Middle Ages. Editions of from five to twenty thousand of historical and scientific works are frequently sold. Let us hope, that in our own country, the diffusion of children's schools, and the superior training given to schoolmasters, will tend to raise these Institutes above mere elementary night schools; and though much remains to be done, the duty of the nation to the children of the poor, so long neglected, is in course of being practically acknowledged.

That Mechanics' Institutes should fail to fulfil the intention of their first promoters to communicate scientific and artistic instruction, was a necessary consequence of the deficiency of the preliminary instruction of the day school, and of the miscellaneous character of the subscribers, a majority of whom required amusing books and lectures, rather than technical instruction. For some years after the establishment of the London Mechanics' Institute, and its contemporaries, the desire to adhere to the objects first aimed at was reluctantly, but gradually, abandoned, as it was found impossible to carry them out. The most

[10] "It is by no means uncommon for professors who have not the attraction of novelty, or the advantage which I happened to enjoy, of coming from a great distance, to command audiences in this Institution as numerous as that above alluded to. The subjects of their discourses are various, such as Natural History, Chemistry, the fine Arts, Natural Theology, and many others. Among my hearers were persons of both sexes, of every station in society, from the most affluent and eminent in the various learned professions to the humblest mechanics, all well dressed and observing the utmost decorum." Page 108.

decided change in their character took place about the time of the agitation of the Reform Bill, 1830 to 1832. Any great political excitement is always unfavourable to the interests of such Institutions, especially among people like our own, with whom politics, in important epochs, possess an absorbing interest. The institutions generally declined, and the establishment of new ones was checked. Had that Reform Bill brought with it a good system of National Education (and never was there a more favourable moment for such a measure, as the subject was popular among all parties), the temporary decline of these Institutes would have been of little moment. Hundreds of thousands of the neglected portion of our population would by this time have received the preparatory training requisite to fit them for perfecting their instruction by means of these Institutes. To revive the prestige of these Institutes, more decided attempts were made to *attract* members by other objects than those first contemplated. Exhibitions of works of art, models, statues, pictures, and machinery, were found to pay well, serving to advertise the Institution, and to diffuse a beneficial and refining influence among the population. Social tea and coffee parties, or as we have since learnt to designate them, *soirées*, became frequent. But the most decided attempt to revolutionise the character of these Institutions, was made by the establishment of "Lyceums" or "People's Institutes." These embraced, as their leading features, news-rooms and a larger provision of light reading. The lectures were very miscellaneous, consisting often of dramatic readings, lectures on elocution, wherein recitations by the lecturer and his pupils formed a prominent part, and musical lectures. They provided instruction for females, and their success in this way is a great encouragement to a similar step now. But the strongest allurement to the operative class was the lowering of the subscription to less than one half of the sum charged by the Manchester and other Institutions.[11] The success of this movement was at first great. In the three Lyceums established at Manchester in 1838, there were together nearly 3,000 members. In the same year the Mechanics' Institute had 1,161 members. The Lyceums and People's Institutes, however, soon declined, and most of them are now extinct. In catering to the taste for amusement, they had formidable rivals in the singing saloons and similar places, and in the provision for instruction, the rate of subscription, when the necessary expenses were met, would leave nothing either to secure permanency or efficiency in the teaching. The influence of their plans was felt after they had ceased. The Mechanics' Institutions, without going to the same extent, introduced objects of a less strictly educational character, to the neglect of others most important, and, what was very much worse, established a scale of fees, which, even if the numbers far exceeded any reasonable anticipation, never could purchase efficient means of instruction.

If Mechanics' Institutes have failed to reach the operative class, so too have they failed in their primary aim,—to convey scientific instruction. This statement may be verified by an actual inspection of the three principal methods employed by them for the diffusion of knowledge.

1. The Library.
2. The Lectures.
3. The Classes.

1st. The Library is the most valuable feature of these Institutes as hitherto conducted. The general complaint of the Committees of these Institutes is the small demand for instructive works as compared with

[11] The subscription paid by the writer (then a boy) to the Manchester Institute was 20*s.* per annum. The Lyceums charged 8*s.* to males and 6*s.* to females, and in some cases took it in half-quarterly, and in even weekly, instalments.

those whose principal aim is amusement. In those Institutes where the directors cater to this taste, the disproportion is enormous. In the Leeds Institute, where very great discretion is exercised over the introduction of books, and especially of those of a light character, the proportion of works of fiction circulated to those of a more solid character is strikingly large, though less than in many less judiciously governed Institutes. The following table will illustrate the character of the reading. In 1852, the library of the Leeds Mechanics' Institute contained 8,629 volumes, and the circulation for that year is thus classified:—

Theology	1,654
Philosophy and Education	1,698
Politics and Statistics	477
History and Biography	7,413
Voyages and Travels	4,435
Poetry and the Drama	1,987
Fine Arts and Literature	4,268
Mathematics	146
Mechanics	704
Chemistry	736
Natural Philosophy	207
Natural History and Gardening	1,055
Medicine and Dietetics	222
Foreign Works	74
	25,076
Fiction	14,090
	39,166
Bound Periodicals	4,040
Unbound ,,	10,325
Total	53,531

Here the fiction and periodical literature is much more than half the whole circulation! The Nottingham Institute contains 5,000 volumes, one-third being works of fiction. The circulation in 1849–50 was 33,000, of which two-thirds consisted of poetry and works of fiction.[12]

[12] History of Adult Education, p. 148.

We cannot go with those who would exclude works of fiction from Mechanics' Institutes. In many their introduction has been strongly resisted, and from some they are still excluded. Such an exclusion appears to us indefensible. One might indeed wish that so large a quantity of "sack" had a little more bread with it; but unless these Institutes had the power of directing the minds of the members into regular study, it is probable that the suppression of light reading would but make fewer instead of better readers. We should also drive many to less carefully selected stores than those on the shelves of the Institute. Moreover, while the undue use of works of imagination is to be deprecated, it must not be forgotten that the imagination has its claims as well as more utilitarian faculties, and that people employed in the active business of life, require their imaginations to be raised and stirred, and are not likely to let them absorb more than their share of attention. The only way of preventing evil from this source, is to exercise great care in the selection and amount of the works introduced, and to supply that training which will make works of a higher character better relishe and appreciated.

The Lecture department of Mechanics' Institutes, so far as conveying any real instruction is concerned, is still less satisfactory than the library. We hear constantly iterated by the managers that "People have got tired of lectures." The reason is, that the people very often derive no real *advantage* from them.

The best lecturing possible, as usually offered in such Institutes, is only a moderately efficient means of instruction. It bears no relation to the previous acquisitions of the auditory. If a word or an illustration is unnoticed or misunderstood, it cannot be repeated or explained, and an important link of the reasoning may be wanting. Very often the lectures even on science, by professional lecturers, ought rather to be called a series of experiments, the reasons and nature of which are scarcely apprehended, still less remembered, by the listener. The lecturer selects a few remarkable experiments, performs them before his audience, most of whom know little or nothing of the *first principles* of the subject; at first they are surprised and pleased, as a child at the wonders of a kaleidoscope or a magic lantern,—they carry home the most vague impressions of what they have heard or seen; but when the novelty has gone, the attraction has ceased. The only sure way to maintain an attendance at lectures, is to make the audience *feel* that they really carry home something worth remembering, that will compensate them for the time spent.

The most valuable lectures are those which partake of the nature of class instruction. The course on any subject should be sufficient in number to enable the teacher to convey adequate information on the principal leading points, and it should be accompanied by either written or oral examinations, and frequent reviews of past lessons. A course of winter lectures so pursued would have results far more valuable than any number of miscellaneous lectures.

The first lectures delivered in Mechanics' Institutes were generally scientific, but owing to the causes alluded to, so soon as the novelty had passed away, dramatic readings, and lectures on music took, their places, which speedily gave way to musical entertainments. At first the lectures were delivered by trained scientific men, and paid for, but very soon the directors found that they could spend the hardly obtained money in ways at least as advantageous to the majority of members, who cared little for lectures, and with more pecuniary profit to the Institute. A course of four lectures would cost twenty or thirty guineas, and be attended by about a twentieth part of the members. Nor would the lectures have a high educational value, disconnected as they were from any class instruction or reading upon the subject of the lectures. Paid lecture were therefore soon abandoned in the majority of Institutes, and unpaid lecture taken instead.[13] These were necessarily selected according to the taste of the lecturer, and generally, there was but one lecture on a subject. Highly valuable as an intellectual pastime for a leisure hour, the positive acquisitions can be but small. The best defence that can be urged for it is, that it is good in default of better, just as reading an entertaining magazine is better than no reading at all. "Of a thousand lectures recently delivered at forty-three Institutes more than half (572) were on literary subjects, about one-third (340) on scientific, and 88 on musical, exclusive of concerts. The number of separate subjects treated of was 549, or on an average there were scarcely two lectures to each subject."[14] The following table illustrates very strikingly the tendency to give up the scientific and practical parts in the lecture department. In the Manchester Institution there were delivered in the fourteen years from 1835 to 1850, the following lectures, thus classified.[15]

	1835–1839.	1840–1844.	1845—1849.
Lectures, Science Physical	235	127	88
„ Science Mental	8	16	2
„ Literature and Education.	53	80	84
„ Fine Arts and the Drama.	99	55	55
	394	278	229

[13] Out of 607 lectures delivered to Yorkshire Institutes in 1852, 144 were paid and 463 unpaid.—*Yorkshire Union Report*, 1852.

[14] Chambers's Papers for the People, article Mechanics' Institutions.

[15] Hist. of Adult Educ. p. 132.

Analysis of Lectures delivered at the Manchester Athenæum, from its establishment in October 1835, to Nov. 1849,—14 years.

	First seven years.	Last seven years.
Lectures, Science Physical.	173	57
„ Science Mental.	——	24
„ Literature Education.	54	108
„ Fine Arts.	125	205
	352	394

The lectures on science grow "small by degrees and beautifully less," nor will any lamentations over this fact avail, unless some means be found of improving the financial position of the Institutes.

And now let us turn to the classes. These best indicate the skill and energy thrown into the management, and the value of the Institute as an educational agency. Occasional lectures, though good as a makeshift, cannot convey much accurate or positive information. The books in the library, though most invaluable to those who know how to read with judgment, too often add little to the real culture of the readers. Few know how to read with profit, and much that is read is often an inchoate jumble of undigested knowledge, oftener, perhaps, a rambling in the regions of dreamland. And though an hour spent with a newspaper, or even with the flimsiest novel ever spun by a professional bookmaker, is vastly superior to many of the ordinary ways of disposing of leisure time, no one can for one moment compare even such occupations with the results of good class instruction. The greater part of reading is of so desultory and rapid a character that little or no permanent impression is left. No facts or principles are accumulated, upon which the mind can draw in future years. All is hazy and indistinct, producing the same sort of feeling that

[16] History of Adult Education, p. 118.

occurs when one tries to revive some long-forgotten incident that we are sure we ought to know something about, and yet cannot distinctly recall. The immense increase of reading in late years, by no means represents a proportionate amount of acquired knowledge, still less does it represent what is more valuable than even large accumulations of knowledge, that discipline of the faculties which strengthens them, and teaches how to turn all acquisitions to advantage. But the action of our institutes has been all in the direction of increasing the amount of *reading*, while *study* has had to take care of itself. It is in the classes we look for the remedy. One who knows well the difficulties of the artisan-student has thus exemplified them. "John Jones, for example, a young man who has been working hard all the day, goes with wearied legs and arms to a lecture-room, to hear a discourse on science; he knows nothing of the subject; he cannot give that close and continued attention necessary to enable him to understand it; he feels drowsy, and speedily falls asleep. He has had no preparation whatever to enable him to profit by the lecture; many of the phrases used are to him quite unintelligible; his mind is vacant or wandering; and if he should resist the temptation to sleep, he comes away with the most vague and confused idea of what the lecturer has been saying. All such persons must be prepared, by the discipline and instruction of classes, to receive the full benefits of lectures. It is in the class-room that the teacher is brought into close contact with ignorance, and enabled to plant knowledge in its place: in it the interest of the pupil is thoroughly awakened: he can commence at any point, he is not hurried over a subject without properly understanding it, his progress may be slow and laborious, but it is certain and sure. The class teacher grapples with ignorance, hand to hand, the lecturer fights with it at a distance. The teacher's labours are severe, arduous, and trying, but the results are seen and certain, the lecturer's labours are comparatively easy, and their results unseen and uncertain. The great object of every attempt at education should be to bring the teacher and the taught into the closest possible contact, so that the knowledge of the one may be easily transferred to the mind of the other. This can be most readily effected in the class-room, seldom and with difficulty in the lecture-hall."[16] It is of little importance to be told that so many members have had so many volumes during the year. It tells us nothing as to the actual amount of knowledge gained. But if we know that so many young men have attended so many lessons in this or that branch of knowledge, and can show that they have mastered what they have been taught, we see that solid and permanent acquisitions are realised. The habit of consecutive thinking, the thorough apprehension of any branch of human knowledge, and the mental discipline which its study involves, can be obtained through systematic instructions of a competent master, and, save by individuals of extraordinary perseverance, in no other way.

The apathy of the operatives to the amelioration of their own mental and social state, is the great difficulty to be overcome; nevertheless it is encouraging to think that when really efficient means of instruction are afforded, they show by their attendance and rapid improvement that they are worthy of every effort made in their behalf. Those who, like the writer, saw "the Classes" in operation in the Manchester Mechanics' Institution so long since as 1830, will remember its large class-rooms crowded with silent and earnest pupils, —so crowded indeed that the teachers had to refuse fresh admissions except as vacancies occurred. What was the secret of this zeal? That the teachers were qualified for their task, and had their heart in the work. The spirit

[14] Chambers' Papers for the People.

which the noble-minded Sir Benjamin Heywood infused into them, they infused into their pupils, who in turn frequently became valuable helps to the Institution. In one of his annual addresses to the members[17], after citing instances of young men who by means of the Institution had raised themselves in the world, he adds, that "they became active instruments of extending to others the advantages of which they have themselves felt the value. They had many instances within their own knowledge. How many members of that Institution were there active and zealous teachers in various Sunday schools in the town? Who were they who, without any emolument, had for four years taken the entire charge of the writing class? Who were they who, in several of the classes, gave their gratuitous assistance to the teachers? Who were they, in the Board of Directors, who devoted their time and their labour to their service? They were men trained up in the Institution."

The youths whose days were spent in the counting-house, the workshops, and the factory, and whose nights were thus devoted to mental culture, have become men, fathers of families, and in some instances employers of labour, scores of whom may thank the instruction they received in the Mechanics' classes for the larger part of the blessings they have enjoyed. The Huddersfield Mechanics' Institute contains about 800 pupils, most of whom are receiving class instruction, much of it elementary, but much also well worthy of a Peoples' College. We know of scarcely another Institute that can compare with it. It reaches the working man and it teaches him. Why? What is the secret? *Efficiency.* It has the advantage of the gratuitous services of the Masters of the Huddersfield College it has a good staff of paid and unpaid teachers, and pretty liberal contributions from the traders and manufacturers of the town.

From a comparison of a large number of Institutes it

[17] February 26. 1835.

appears that the attendance at evening classes comprises less than a sixth of the whole number of members.[17a] The classes even for elementary instruction have not increased in proportion to the number of members, and those for more advanced studies still less so. The progress that has been made in this department in the largest Institute in the Kingdom—that of Leeds—is an epitome of the Institutes everywhere.

Year.	Total Members.	Actual Average Attendance.			Total.
		Drawing Class.	Mathematic Class.	Chemical Class.	
1839	332	34	36	19	89
1853	2,166	35	24	13	72

The proportion for these three most important classes being 17 less than it was thirteen years ago, while the number of subscribers has increased nearly seven fold. In the Manchester Mechanics' Institute the number of pupils in the classes in 1836 was 787, and thirteen years later 706.

The instruction of females was probably not contemplated by the earlier founders of Mechanics' Institutes, and the omission has certainly not been since greatly remedied. Out of 86 Institutes[18], containing 14,962 members, only 1,520, or one-tenth of the whole, were females. This great disparity may in part be attributable to the erroneous notions prevailing on the subject of the true position of Woman, and especially amongst the labouring classes. If in superior stations Woman is too often considered as an elegant toy, in the lower ranks she is too frequently treated merely as a domestic slave. In the first she must learn the lighter accomplishments,

[17a] The actual attendance at 59 institutes giving class instruction, and containing 11,813 members, is 2,810. It appears from the return that even of the small proportion of members (under 1-4th of the whole) attending evening classes, 4-5ths are in the elementary classes, as reading, writing, and arithmetic.—*Yorkshire Union Report*, 1853.

[18] Report of the Yorkshire Union of Mechanics' Institutes for 1852.

whatever else she may acquire; in the lower her edcuation, still more emphatically than that of the stronger sex, is left to take care of itself.

> "Man, oft to Man unjust,
> Is always so to Woman."

The elevation of Woman is too large a subject to enter upon here; but it is obvious that many of the arguments which apply to the education of the male sex, apply with equal force to the female, while there are some reasons which give the latter even a more imperative claim. If a woman is not cultivated so as to be a companion for her husband, she is but his drudge. True it is, that economy, order, cleanliness, and other household virtues, are possible without the possession of much book learning; but there are other qualities not less essential to domestic happiness than these. Good temper, and at least moderate intelligence, are equally requisite. We know instances, and they are not uncommon, when from want of knowing how to improve a leisure hour, women of the labouring class become disagreeably clean: cooking, washing, scrubbing, and rubbing, from Monday morning till Saturday night, their whole time is devoted to the worship (on their knees) of their household gods the furniture and fire-irons. Although this is a less evil than a literary slattern, yet for a human being gifted with faculties for far higher purposes, this is surely a melancholy perversion. Or sometimes want of better knowledge causes a large portion of time to be wasted in stupid gossip, at others it exhibits itself in an undue and disproportionate love of dress and finery. Persons who have visited manufacturing towns must have often been struck with the incongruity between the elegantly dressed females and their coarse tone, language, and manners. Nothing manifests so strikingly the direction which our *progress* has taken this last few years. One is almost tempted to parody Hood's lines and say, —

> Alas! that dress should be so cheap,
> And common sense so dear.

The coarseness which the conditions of their birth and training, uncounteracted by any superior influence, too often induce, acts even more disastrously upon the character of their children than upon the happiness of the husband. The greatest educators have confessed, that all they could do was nothing compared with the influence of the mother upon the child. The greatest men the world has yet produced, have (with singular unanimity) traced the germs of their greatness to maternal influence. Pondering this truth, so notorious as to be commonplace, let any one visit the cottages and the small streets of our large towns; let him see the filth and squalor in which the children are revelling, with the fortunate unconsciousness of childhood; let him listen to the frequent language of passion, and witness, as he often may, the brutal violence of personal chastisement towards these, the men and women of the next generation,—he will not wonder that with such a preparation at home, backed by the penny theatre and the casino abroad, the boy or girl leaves the parental roof as soon as they earn a few shillings a week, and set up as precocious men and women, even before childhood is well completed. It may be objected that as the occupations pursued by men are so much more varied than those pursued by women, the latter could derive no advantage from many of those studies which are essential to the success of the former. We reply that there is a distinction between that general culture which *all* ought to have, and the special cultivation suited to particular pursuits. To the former there is surely no reason why women should not lay claim equally with men. And as to the latter, we think that for many departments of industry and commerce, women are as well adapted as men, but from which they are cruelly and unjustly excluded. In France there are various employments much more open to women than they are with us. Speaking on this subject, John Stuart Mill justly remarks, "A change which lies in the direct line of the best tendencies of the time is the opening of industrial occupations freely to both sexes. The same reasons which make it no longer necessary that the poor should depend on the rich, make it equally unnecessary that women should depend on men, and the best which justice requires is, that law and custom should not enforce dependence, (when the co-relative protection has become superfluous) by ordaining that a woman who does not happen to have a provision by inheritance, shall have scarcely any means open to her of gaining a livelihood, except as a wife and mother. Let women who prefer that occupation, adopt it; but that there should be no option, no other *carrière* possible, for the great majority of women, except in the humble departments of life, is one of those social injustices which call loudest for remedy."[19] It is gratifying to observe that in the new schools of practical art, we are beginning to repair our injustice. Of the five special classes established in Marlborough House for the purpose of applying the new system of drawing to the practical purposes of production, there are in operation female classes for Wood Engraving and Chromo-Lithography. The class for Designs for Woven Fabrics and Paper Hangings, and that for China Paintings, are open to both sexes, and only that for metal work is restricted to male students. If such establishments are promoted, we shall not find well-educated females doomed to become half-starved governesses, or compelled, if following some light industrial employment, to hand over to some middle man half of their hard-won earnings, to conceal "the degradation" (as they have erroneously been taught to deem it) of earning their maintenance by honest industry. Assuredly, if other departments of industry had been open to women, many of those horrors would have been prevented, which

[19] Political Economy, vol. ii. book iv. chap. vii. sect. 3.

Hood has recorded in "thoughts that breathe, and words that burn," and which Sidney Herbert and others have so nobly stept in to remedy.

Once allow that women have equal rights with men to instruction, and that its bestowal is of equal urgency, and the practical difficulties will melt away. Where this conviction is not entertained, molehills will swell into mountains, and nothing can be done. We have heard worthy people who objected to both sexes visiting the same Institution at the same time — they would go home together, and that would be improper, perhaps dangerous! They forget that places of worship and large workshops, where both sexes are employed, are open to the same objection. In many instances both sexes attend the lectures, and though convenience would dictate that where practicable the male and female classes should be separate, we have seen classes attended by both where the strictest decorum prevailed, probably more than would have been maintained by the separation of the sexes. In large towns it would be quite practicable to have a distinct Institute for the class instruction of females, while the two Institutes might, for greater economy, enjoy the same lectures and library. Small towns would not afford such a division. In Huddersfield, where exists, as Dr. Hook says, "the only Mechanics' Institute which has any pretension to meet the wants of the people," the inhabitants can boast of a Female Institute. The following report, furnished to us by the Secretary of that Institute, is interesting in several points of view: —

"The Huddersfield Female Educational Institute has been established since January 1847, and it was probably the first, as it has been the most successful, of the kind ever established in this country. The management of the Institute consists of a committee composed of all the lady teachers and of such of the gentlemen teachers or subscribers as may be elected thereto by the

Institute. The pupils also select six of their own number who form part of the Committee. The class of females enjoying the benefits of the Institute is principally composed of factory operatives, milliners, and dressmakers, with a few domestic servants. The numbers upon the books of the Institution will be about three-fourths above the average attendance; that is to say, we have about two hundred pupils, with an average attendance of fifty. The subjects taught embrace reading, writing, arithmetic, grammar, composition, geography, history, and plain sewing. The efforts made to attend the classes by some of the pupils are very great, and involve not a few sacrifices. They come two miles, and in some instances more. The ages of the pupils vary from eleven to forty; the majority of them being over eighteen years. A system of regularly visiting the absentees is kept up by the Secretary; and he is convinced that, as a means of obtaining information and securing the interest of the pupils, as also the co-operation of the parents in affording them the opportunity of attending, it is far more important than any other, except that of good and regular teaching.

"With the exception of the secretary and one assistant paid teacher, the instruction imparted is by gratuitous teachers, whose exertions in this particular Institution have been beyond all praise. A feeling of sympathy has sprung up between the teacher and the pupil which has not terminated with their connexion with the Institute, but has continued after the marriage and settlement of the pupil in some instances, and after their removal from the town in others. The Institution has also been the means of introducing deserving pupils to suitable situations, thereby rendering a material service both to employer and employed. This Institution is, like all others of an educational character dependent solely upon voluntary effort for their support,—subject to the most trying difficulties both in respect to the falling off in its funds in times of commercial difficulty or public indifference, and also from the difficulty of obtaining efficient gratuitous teachers. These difficulties have indeed been so great at times as to lead to very serious discussions as to the propriety of abandoning the Institution."[20]

We commend this account to those heads of families who, considering their female servants as the "greatest plague in life," try to mitigate it by changing their plagues twelve times per annum. We have heard them express their horror of servants who could read, and the guilt of such an accomplishment was only surpassed by the depravity of being able to write. Perhaps such gifts, employed in perusing penny trash, or copying stupid poetry, and writing foolish love letters, are not very profitable endowments; but if our domestic servants could enjoy such real instruction as is given in the Huddersfield Female Institute, they would know better how to use their leisure, unless it is a mistake to speak of this class of the community enjoying leisure at all. We have tried the system of ignorance, and *that* fails; let us try *that* of knowledge and kind treatment, and see if that will work a change. Perhaps it might. Perhaps they might turn out, after all, to manifest the ordinary qualities of human beings. At least it is worth an experiment.

We thus see that the deficiencies of our Mechanics' Institutes, notwithstanding all their merits, have been many and serious. In the next two chapters we shall endeavour to point out the remedy. These Institutes have overlooked half of the population altogether, and have scarcely touched as yet the other half. They

20 Had it not been for the disinterested benevolence of one of its oldest supporters, and its founder, Samuel Kell, Esq., now of Bradford, that measure must have been taken; but this gentleman has during the past year contributed in donations and subscriptions more than one half in amount of the whole.

have both wanted guidance as to the objects to be pursued, and the means to obtain them. Large numbers of them, established for the work of self-improvement, were formed solely by those who required instruction, unaided by any one who could assist them in the choice of studies, of books, or of lectures. If any superficial, but fluent speaker, visiting their neighbourhood, told them that by means of his sixpenny catechism on Phrenology, they could acquire a whole world of mental science, besides getting a thorough knowledge of the characters of all their acquaintance merely by feeling their bumps, no wonder that a large class would be at once formed for the study. Another might promise them a royal road to all sorts of knowledge, by learning a few arbitrary signs, and a class would forthwith be formed for *that.* A third would have a system of mnemonics, which would enable the learner to remember everything. The system might be open to the slight objection that it was itself more difficult to retain, than even the facts it was meant to hold tight in the treacherous brain of the learner. No matter — a class for the study was forthwith formed. No one can estimate the amount of time and energy wasted in such abortive attempts to reap the fruits of knowledge, without sowing the seed. The working man requires guidance, both how to learn and what to learn. In the words of one whose whole life has been devoted to the work of promoting education[21], "Mechanics' Institutions have rather pointed the way to Adult Education, and given form and currency to the impression of its necessity, than supplied the want. As solid educational establishments they have yet done little, — they have immensely disseminated the feeling of the want of education, they have not laid their hands to the work. They have given lectures

[21] Thomas Wilson, Esq., M. A.

which imply knowledge — rather than taught how to acquire it — essays on literature and science, rather than classes to train up men to the realisation for themselves of the blessings of literature and science — 'they have played round the head' of the mechanic, and awakened a momentary flash across his brain, but they have 'come not near his heart,' nor lightened up in himself — in his mind a fire, that will supply him with constant warmth and light. This they can do, and this they must be made to do."

CHAPTER II.

OBJECTS AND METHODS OF ADULT INSTRUCTION.

MECHANICS' Institutes, to answer their end, must become more educational and practical. Miscellaneous lectures and general readings are not *study*. A man, after listening to such lectures, and reading good books during a whole life, might not understand a simple science, or be master of a single department of human knowledge. His information, like his reading, would be crude, undigested, not always available when wanted, and very little of it probably connected with his own particular vocation. It would also be much less in amount than if he had applied the same time in regular and systematic study. No patent process has yet been discovered, no royal road yet found out, which will impart to a man the power of knowledge, without going through the labour needful to acquire it.

Education is not an affair of childhood and youth, it is the business of the whole life. The infant and day school but commence education. The education that should cease with youth would soon pass away as a dream. It is found that even the ability to read and write is lost in multitudes of instances simply for want of opportunity for using it. This is the case equally with more advanced knowledge.

What, then, is the instruction which Mechanics' Institutes *should* offer to the working classes? The answer is twofold. There is an instruction which they should receive to fit them for the position of members of a civilised community, and there is an instruction specially adapted to their individual vocations. We shall offer a few remarks on each of these.

Some good people are apt to imagine that when we have furnished the mind with the instruments of knowledge, reading and writing, we are at the end of our task. They might just as well look upon a knife and fork as a dinner. They say, when a knowledge of these elements has not secured us from the consequences of ignorance, "Look how education has failed." The same kind of mistake is made in the education of the superior ranks. It is fancied that because a man knows the name of a stool in half a dozen languages, he must needs know how to sit upon one. We claim for the working man more than a mere knowledge of reading and writing, indispensable as these are. "If," as George Combe remarks, "the working classes have been created by Providence merely to toil and pay taxes, to eat, sleep, and transmit existence to future generations, a limited education may suffice; but if they are born with the full faculties of moral, intellectual, and religious beings; if they are as capable, when instructed, of studying the works of God, of obeying his laws, of loving him and admiring his institutions, as any class of the community; in short, if they are rational beings, capable of all the duties, and susceptible of all the enjoyments which belong to the rational character, then no education is sufficient for them which leaves any portion of their highest powers waste and unproductive."

The working man ought to know something of the world in which he lives, its physical character, its geological history, its relation to the other orbs of our solar system, and of that sidereal system of aggregated worlds in which it is but an atom. The man who is once admitted to this august temple of the universe, where "glory is thronging on glory and grandeur on grandeur," will not readily stoop to poorer pleasures. Whatever is mean and base will appear still more so. He ought to be made acquainted with the leading facts in the history of his race, the rise and fall of empires, and the conditions of the social system in which he lives. "A man," says D'Israeli, "who knows nothing but the history of the passing hour, who knows nothing of the history of the past, but that a certain person whose brain was as vacant as his own occupied the same house as himself, who in a moment of despondency or of gloom has no hope in the morrow because he has read nothing that has taught him that the morrow has any changes—that man, compared with him who has read the most ordinary abridgment of history, or the merest philosophical speculation, is as distinct and different an animal as if he had fallen from some other planet, was influenced by a different organisation, working for a different end, and hoping for a different result." He ought to know the wonderful laws of his own body, the unerring compensations which attend upon obedience to these laws, and the punishments that wait upon their neglect. He should know the relation in which he stands to the laws of the world, and taking his happiness into his own keeping, exercise that prudence and self-control essential to his welfare, and fulfil those duties which devolve upon him as a moral and accountable agent. "The great work of mankind on earth," says an eloquent American writer, "is to live a manly life, to raise, develop and enjoy every limb of the body, every faculty of the spirit, each in its just proportion, all in their proper place, duly co-ordinating what is merely personal and for the present time with what is universal and for ever."

To take an illustration from a single branch of knowledge, let us suppose that any means existed for conveying to the mass of the community the teachings of physiology,—not the minutiæ and technicalities which are suited only for the medical man, but the broad generalisation of the science. Suppose that the injurious effects of stimulus and excitement upon the system were pointed out. Might we not hope to diminish the number of young men, and even youths, who may be seen in large numbers every Sunday, and at their period of leisure, debilitating their constitutions by smoking and drinking, and forming habits which but few will ever break off. What a world of folly and ill-health would be spared the young women, if they could once be made to understand the importance of permitting the lungs to have their proper breathing space. How much might be done to promote general cleanliness, and consequent health, if all knew the functions of the skin. And though mere knowledge is not invariably an antidote to sin, where the moral feelings are perverted, there is no doubt that a large proportion of secret vice — vice whose existence is indicated by every newspaper, and placarded on every wall, furnishing the means of support to hundreds of quacks, — would be, if not entirely prevented, at least materially checked, were our youth rightly instructed, and noble pursuits made the employment of the leisure hour. It is not labour which cuts off our working population before half the allotted span of life is over. It is not even poverty, intense as that has been in periods of distress. Elixired and cordialled in infancy by ignorant mothers, uncontrolled by the authority of parents while young, surrounded by the most pernicious examples, their growth is stunted and their strength destroyed even before they reach maturity. Want of better objects of pursuit, and utter ignorance of themselves and of the natural laws — these are the causes which, above all others, produce the mass of disease and demoralisation witnessed in our large towns.

There is also the special training of the artisan — that which is to better fit him for his "art, trade, or calling." We are learning to look on labour, not as a disgrace, but as a necessity for all men, — a training for the faculties. We are beginning to see that ignorance is not the necessary, but only the accidental, associate of labour: in the conducting of the business of a manufacturer or a merchant there is as much art as in many of those pursuits of literature and science which bring fame and reputation. Is not the knowledge which produces from the cotton pod or the fleece a beautiful piece of calico or worsted as great as that required to master Greek and Latin conjugations? We should honour *such* studies indeed; but why science, which serves the wants of millions, should not hold up its head as proudly as that which ministers but to few,—why it should not have its schools, it colleges, and its universities,—is only explicable upon the hypothesis that we have not quite emerged from the errors and darkness of feudalism.

In earlier days we have seen small states of but a few thousands of inhabitants exercising a larger influence than empires with as many millions, owing to the superior *arts* and *civilisation* of the former. The superiority of Great Britain over other nations lies in her manufacturing and commercial greatness. It is this which has enabled an insignificant island to conquer and unite vast empires to itself, and to maintain its rank among the greatest nations of Europe. If our ability to manufacture as well and as cheaply as other nations is lessened, if other nations advance at a faster ratio than ourselves in the arts of industry, not only will our superiority be endangered, but our very existence. We have no outlying regions to fall back upon; the sea, which limits our shores and bears our rich vessels to every clime, would become our curse. Hitherto, it is true, our natural advantages,—our mines of tin, and coal, and iron,—have enabled us to distance all competitors; and we naturally enough imagine that the superiority already acquired we must inevitably maintain, even though we make no more efforts in the future than we have done in the past. The sooner we rid ourselves of this delusion the better. It is not a superiority in natural advantages which will longer secure our supremacy, but the skill and ability to use them. "As locomotion improves," says Dr. Lyon Playfair[22], "the local advantages of the country to which the raw material is indigenous become of less importance as an element in production; and industrial competition depends more upon labour, — the second factor, — than upon the first. This is certainly the case, or raw cotton could not be imported from America, to be exported as calico; malachite, sand, and wool, could not come from Australia, to go back as copper, glass, and broad-cloth; nor could Dutch madder reach us, to return to Holland as printed ginghams; or horse-hair and fat from Buenos Ayres and Russia, to be returned as hair-cloth and soap. All this shows that the superiority of labour in one country does more than compensate for the disadvantages arising from increased cost in the raw material."

The increase of the applications of mechanical and chemical science to the arts of life, diminishes in the same degree the value of unskilled labour. The nation which possesses the largest number of skilled artizans, capable of availing themselves of the aids which science lends to industry, will, other things being equal, be the richest nation. "The fact is every day more apparent," says the same writer, "that mere muscular labour, in the present state of the world, is little better than raw material, and that both these are sinking in value as elements of production, while nervous or intellectual labour is constantly rising. The whole of industrial competition is now resolved into a struggle to obtain a *maximum* effect by a *minimum* expenditure of power." We have carried *division* of labour to extreme limits, we want the *synthesis* of labour, the bringing together the knowledge required in each department of industry, so

22 Lecture on Industrial Education on the Continent, at the Museum of Practical Geology, page 4.

that he who labours in one may know what aid he can obtain from the others.

What have we been doing to cultivate the intelligence of our workmen and to unite science with industry? The only institutions that even *professed* such an end have been our Mechanics' Institutes; and we have seen what moderate aims they proposed, and how very far they fell short even of these. But while we have thus been neglectful, almost every country in Europe has been actively engaged in establishing Institutes for industrial education. In Prussia, Saxony, Austria, Bavaria, there are, in addition to the primary schools so plentifully supplied, a large number of trade schools, conveying instruction in those branches of knowledge which have the most intimate connexion with the industrial arts. In France they have the Ecole Polytechnique, Ecole des Mines, Ecole Centrale des Arts et Manufactures, and the Conservatoire des Arts et Metiers.[23] Dr. Lyon Playfair tells us, "that the general character of all secondary education in Germany is tending towards giving instruction in the wants of the nineteenth century," that "industrial schools are increasing abroad, and that the number of their pupils is constantly augmenting," and that they are already manifesting their influence on industry. Speaking on the chemical principles involved in the manufactures of the exhibition, he thus warns us:—"The influence of capital may purchase you for a time foreign talent. Our Manchester calico printers may, and do, use foreign talent, both in management and design. Our silversmiths and diamond-setters may, and do, depend much upon foreign talent in art and foreign skill in execution; but is all this not a suicidal policy, which must have, not for the individual manufacturer, who wisely buys

[23] For fuller particulars respecting these various continental industrial schools, see Dr. Playfair's Lecture on Industrial Education on the Continent.

the best talent wherever he can get it, but for the nation, which, careless of the education of her sons, sends our capital abroad as a premium to that intellectual progress which, in our present apathy, is our greatest danger?"[24]

In those Institutions situated in the rural districts,—and with proper arrangements there is scarcely a village but might possess one,—the "industrial instruction" communicated might exercise an important influence in increasing the application of science to agriculture. Important as the knowledge of chemistry is to the artizans of the town employed in dyeing, bleaching, and other trades, it is equally so to the husbandman. "It performs a part, indeed," says the Edinburgh Review, "in almost every process, throws light upon every appearance, explains the qualities and uses of all the materials which the husbandman works with or produces, and aims at removing the greater part of the difficulties which lie in his way. The culture of the land, the manuring of the crops, their value when reaped, the feeding and treatment of stock, the manufacture and management of butter and cheese, have all been made the subjects of analytical investigation in the laboratory."[25] Speaking of the prospects of agriculture, the same writer observes, "It is from the aids of science, hitherto so much undervalued, that British agriculture is to draw new strength. If other nations have outstripped her in any part, she, by the use of the same means, may surely outstrip her present self." Mr. Mechi, whose merits as a scientific agriculturist are well known, attributes the unprofitable state of agriculture to "two causes—want of knowledge and want of capital, and that it is unprofitable more frequently from want of knowledge than deficiency of capital. The remedy for these evils is the communi-

[24] Lectures on the Results of the Great Exhibition, p. 196. See Appendix B.

[25] Edinburgh Review, Oct. 1849, page 363., Article on Agriculture and Science.

cation of agricultural knowledge to both landlords and tenants."[26] Much preliminary information might be given and a basis laid for larger operations by the circulation of books, the formation of classes, and the delivery of systematic courses of lectures in the rural districts. Make scientific agriculture a department of the New Industrial University, let its professors and teachers visit our village institutes and libraries and organise the means of instruction we speak of. By being made the medium of communicating practical and valuable information, these Institutes would assume their due importance in the eyes of the farmer and the landlord instead of meeting, as at present, contempt and opposition. The value of the knowledge taken on its lowest grounds would repay ten times the cost of communicating it. No protective duty would raise the value of agriculture so much as the improved intelligence of those who pursue it. In the Report on Public Libraries it is stated that in the county of Wigtown, and in many other places in Scotland, when agriculture was in a comparatively backward state, there was a great improvement in husbandry there, chiefly through the influence of such libraries and clubs.[27] What a valuable preparation to the emigrant settler would such information prove. How much improvement even in other channels would such instruction draw along with it.

[26] "The knowledge will be best promoted and diffused by agricultural schools or colleges with farms attached, on the principle of that excellent one now establishing at Cirencester. There should be one or more such establishments in every county in the United Kingdom. There should be agricultural endowed colleges of the first order, under authority, where students should qualify by superior practical and theoretic knowledge, passing their examinations and obtaining their agricultural diplomas the same as in law or medicine. Such qualified individuals would thus spread over the country agricultural schools and farms, advantages alike to themselves and the rising generation of farmers, who would imbibe sound theoretical and practical instruction." (Letters on Agricultural Improvement, page 90.) For a very excellent article on County Colleges of Agriculture, by D. F. Duppa, Esq., see the 3rd publication of the Central Society of Education.

[27] Report, page 253.

The meeting together, not merely to bargain or to brawl in the village public-house, but for higher intellectual purposes, would, to those whose opportunities for meeting are so rare, have of itself a civilising tendency. The landlord, the farmer, the labourer would be brought into more intimate relations with each other. Many other lessons besides those which relate to the management of manures would insensibly and inevitably be drawn in therewith. Other books would be read, other lectures listened to, and the "agricultural mind" would not lag so much in the rear of the rest of the world. If we cannot make the labourer rich in material wealth, we can make the little means he possesses go much further than it would; and, above all, we can make him rich in the solid advantages of knowledge, and the pure and refined pleasures which spring from its pursuit. "Many a rough hind," says Sir J. Herschel, "on Highland hills, is as familiar with the Paradise Lost or the works of his great national historians as with his own sheephook." Deficient as the manufacturing towns are in educational facilities, the presence of a middle and upper class helps to keep up a higher tone of intellectual life even among those who share but little of its advantages. There is also the newspaper, the cheap publication, the contact of mind with mind — all have to a certain degree an educative influence. All these things are denied to large portions of our agricultural population.

The pure and ennobling scenes of nature lose more than half their influence for want of culture. And it is among them chiefly that every absurd superstition lingers longest, and where the wildest fanaticism finds most numerous dupes. When some fifteen years ago Mad Thom played his vagaries in Kent, and made numbers of the peasantry believe him to be Jesus Christ, — when eight of his disciples, *martyrs to ignorance*, lost their lives by the bullets of the military, it was found that the state of knowledge amply accounted for the result. It was proved how little the ability to "read a little in the Testament," which so many of these dupes possessed, was able to guard against the grossest delusions. In the cottages, not a Penny Magazine or a single cheap periodical was to be seen. In Herne Hill, one of the scenes of this tragedy, it was found that, "of fifty-one families examined, seven parents only ever opened a book after the labours of the day were closed. To the inquiry, "How they passed their time in the long winter evenings," the answer in most cases was, "About home, doing sometimes one thing, sometimes another; but most times, going early to bed for want of something to do."[28] In Dunkirk and Boughton, adjacent villages, the facts were of the same character. But, indeed, most of the agricultural districts were in the same predicament; and, notwithstanding the progress made in the last fifteen years, they are so still. If we have not such events as the Mad Thom tragedy oftener, it is because such personages are scarce, rather than because there is any want of opportunity to play their vagaries. Let but a fanatic Mormon apostle arise in such places, and present daily experience shows that he would find plenty of adherents.

What, then, is meant by Industrial Education? Is it designed to form amateur workshops, where the practical manipulations required in each trade shall be taught? Such a plan is neither desirable nor possible. Dr. Birkbeck's first attempts partook of this character, but were speedily changed for the communication of scientific instruction by means of lectures. And in the Edinburgh School of Arts, where at first it was intended to teach the Arts in detail, "it was found best to limit

[28] For this, and other information, see Report of F. Liardet on the State of the Peasantry in the County of Kent. Third publication of the Central Society of Education.

the lectures to the general principle of those sciences which are of universal application to the Arts."[29] Speaking of industrial instruction upon the Continent, Dr. Playfair says of the Trade Institute of Berlin, "The chief peculiarity of this Institution was its being originally confined to the workmen, who, in addition to the principles of their trade, were even taught their mechanical craft in extensive workshops. It is now, however, acknowledged that this was an error, and that the practice of an art can only be learned satisfactorily in the workshops of industry."

And, again, in some general observations on the continental systems of industrial instruction, he says,—"In all of them there are differences with regard to the mode of giving instruction; but they are almost uniform in the feeling, that the object of industrial schools is only to teach a pupil how to become an intelligent manufacturer, without attempting to make him one. They content themselves with communicating to him a knowledge of the principles upon which his technical art depends; but for its practice he must go to the workshops of industry. Some of the institutions, as, for example, the "Trade Institute of Berlin," endeavoured at one time to teach practice in workshops attached to the institution; but this plan, as might have been anticipated, was found to be of little advantage; and it is now abandoned by almost all the schools, only one or two being still found hovering on the outskirts of this error.

* * * *

"We do not think that such schools can substitute a practical training in the workshops, the factory, or the office of the engineer; but we do think that a producer possessing a knowledge of natural forces will become a practical man in a shorter time than without it, and

[29] Lord Brougham, Edinburgh Review, October, 1824, p. 112.

that he will know how to turn his practice to the best account.

* * * *

"The promoters of industrial instruction do not, therefore, offer it as a substitute for practical training, but consider it to be a means by which the latter can be made more efficacious. They do not think that the seed will grow, unless the land is well tilled by the practical farmer; but they offer to manure the land first, and the ploughing in the manure will enrich the soil, and render it more productive."[30]

No Mechanics' Institute could advantageously attempt to carry out instruction in the special details and manipulations of the different arts. But it can and should afford the instruction requisite to understand their principles. It could not teach the paper-stainer or the house-painter his trade; but the same teacher, the same text-book, the same class-room, could furnish instruction to them both at the same time as to the principles and harmony of colours. The chemical teacher could not convey instruction in all the arts, for they are numberless, which involve applications of chemical principles; but having given his pupils a practical acquaintance with the general principles of his science, he enables them to make for themselves those applications of its truths which a particular business requires. The student who has learnt to draw from the flat and the round, and has acquired facility in the use of the pencil, will not find much difficulty in turning his skill to that department of drawing most requisite for him. He who has thoroughly acquired the knowledge of numbers, will find it equally available in calculating the prices of cotton or of corn. The same practical geometry measures equally the size of a field and the distance of suns and stars. And, above all, there is obtained from the mental discipline which study brings, something far

[30] Dr. Playfair's Lectures on Industrial Education on the Continent, p. 32.

more valuable than the subject-matter wherein it is engaged,—a strong and self-reliant intellect that can adapt itself to the varying emergencies of life.

It is impossible to lay down a programme of study, suitable to all classes of Institutes, since it would have to be modified in a thousand various ways, according to the locality, the numbers willing to partake of the advantages of particular classes, and the means available for the purpose. Besides, it is to be hoped, that with the progress of education, a continually improving standard of adult education will be formed. No system of adult education can supply the want, or remedy the defects of early education, though it may mitigate their evils. In the first instance, the great deficiency is of classes for instruction in reading, writing, and arithmetic. If we wish the Institutes to embrace the factory-worker and the day-labourer, the instruction offered must descend even to this point. Indeed, the staple of what little class-instruction is now offered in the Institutes is but the knowledge of these elements. Though much remains to be done to convey elementary instruction to adults, the progress of education during the last few years, especially among the better paid class of operatives, opens out opportunities for far more advanced studies; nor do we know a better model at present than the Edinburgh School of Arts, of which Dr. Hudson says, that it is the only establishment in Britain deserving the title of a "People's College." To gain one of its diplomas, a course of study must be gone through, requiring an attendance of three years. The first year is devoted to mathematics, including arithmetic and algebra; the second year to chemistry, and the third to natural philosophy. In addition to these classes, the Institute comprises classes for drawing, modelling, English grammar, and French. Classes were also formed for natural history, political economy, and singing, but these have been discontinued. There is nothing in this programme which might not at once be adopted in all Institutes in the large towns, and, in part, in many of those of the smaller ones, if only the means existed of providing adequate instruction. We do not offer the programme of the Edinburgh School of Arts as the best, we only say that experience has shown that it is a practicable one. "This Institute," says Dr. Hudson, "has in the 28 years of its existence improved the material and moral condition of no less than 12,000 persons who have received instruction in its classes. To its classes for drawing and modelling, several men who are eminent as sculptors and architects in various parts of the kingdom owe their position in life."

If it were hereafter contemplated to establish a superior order of Industrial Colleges, such a course of study would form an excellent preparation for them. Dr. Playfair complains, that in the School of Mines in London, the pupils come untrained in science, and that the time is spent in "teaching its elements instead of its applications. In the trade schools of Germany, pupils are not generally admitted into the upper technical class of mechanics, physics, or chemistry, unless they have passed examinations in integral and differential calculus."

In drawing, the new School of Practical Art is attempting to provide that elementary instruction which will hereafter enable our adult schools to embrace more advanced stages of study. For some years our deficiencies in artistic taste have been notorious. When our manufacturers required pattern-designers, they employed those who were trained abroad, but more often they made use of the patterns obtained from thence. The attempts to remedy this evil gave rise to the schools of design. It would be unjust to say that the schools of design have failed, but owing to defects in their management, what they have done has been at an absurdly extravagant cost compared with their results. In the new schools of art, a better organization of these schools will be attempted. The teacher, who has to pass an examination to show that he understands and can teach the system of study, will visit the day schools, and give instruction to all the children. That this mode of procedure will largely diffuse habits of correct taste among the community, cannot be doubted, and to diffuse such a taste is as important as to have tasteful artizans, who can in their productions, appropriately minister to it. As Mr. Cole observes, "The manufacturer simply obeys his demand; if it be for gaudy trash he supplies it; if for subdued refinement, he will supply it too." While an improved taste will be diffused by introducing drawing on correct principles into all schools, those pupils who show superior abilities will, under the arrangements, have facilities furnished for carrying on their artistic culture to that degree of perfection requisite to fit them for furnishing the highest assistance which manufacturers may demand from art. They will furnish the superior workmen to those trades where artistic skill is demanded.

The first essential of any such improvement in the operations of our Mechanics' Institutes, is *the provision of properly qualified and properly paid teachers.* Without this condition, even the proper elementary instruction of our institutes cannot be supplied. The smallness of the number of scholars in adult evening classes arises from want of teachers rather than scarcity of those who need teaching and are willing to be taught. Teachers for elementary instruction there would be little difficulty in obtaining, at least in large towns, if there were funds to pay them; but the Reports of the Country Institutes are filled with complaints of their inability to obtain teachers. For instruction of a more advanced character, this difficulty might amount to an impossibility.

Of course the character of the class-instruction offered, must partake of the inadequacy of the means of its communication. Mr. Thomas Hogg, formerly the secretary of the Lancashire and Cheshire Union of

Mechanics' Institutes, says of it, — "Each class is to a great extent isolated from another, and their existence sometimes depends on the fluctuating tastes and wants, often the caprice of the members. There is no regular course of study through which a student is either required or expected to pass. To working men, the classes often present few, if any advantages, except the acquirement of elementary knowledge; and those really desirous of obtaining in the Mechanics Institution a knowledge of the principles of their trades, seldom find that knowledge there."[31] "The system," observes Dr. Hudson, "of instruction pursued, appears to have been based on the rule of teaching the largest number with the least possible trouble. The pupil, in entering the Institution, selects the class himself, in which he is placed mechanically at the desk, before his slate or copybook, and, from the effects of the discipline, fitted rather for children than for men, he soon loses all interest in the study which led him to sacrifice his leisure in the attainment of solid education."

The cause of such a state of things lies obviously in the want of a properly qualified teacher, who can only be obtained by being properly paid. We have no objection to gratuitous teachers, but they must always be in a subordinate capacity: devotion to the task will help to make up for many deficiencies; but teaching is an art, and the amateur who takes it up, unconscious of its difficulties, betrays his unfitness for the task. It is singular, that the pursuit of the highest difficulty and importance is that which is least esteemed. Education is the only science which every one thinks he knows without learning,—the only art which nobody seems to think requires an apprenticeship.

Dr. Hook, in his excellent Lecture on Institutes for Adult Instruction[32], has thus stated the objection to

[31] Suggestions for the Improvement of Mechanics' Institutes, May, 1851.

[32] Delivered at the Church Institute, Wakefield, October, 1851.

gratuitous teachers:—"Gratuitous teachers cannot be depended upon; and they require to be viewed rather as assistants than as principals. If you look to gratuitous teachers, you must be seeking an inferior article: for intellectual power, when duly cultivated, has its marketable value; and he who offers his service gratuitously, would make teaching his primary occupation, if he felt himself qualified for the rank of a professor. Or, if he be a man of superior and cultivated mind, he is engaged in some other pursuit, and his class, though an important, is still with him a secondary, consideration, to which he gives the fag-end of his time and an already exhausted mind. In a teacher is requisite not only a competent knowledge of his subject, but an aptness to teach, which can only be acquired, generally speaking, by those who make teaching their sole occupation and study. We demand for the working classes the best article; and the best article you cannot afford."

Next in importance to the teacher come the *tools to work with*, under which head we include a library of reference, and the class-books, models, and apparatus used in instruction. The school library of reference should be distinct from that of general reference and circulation, and its use limited to those who either were engaged in the classes or had passed through them. It should contain the leading works on the special subjects of the classes, and the latest additions made thereto. The large and expensive works on architecture, mechanics[33], chemistry, would be there, and if confined to those who really wanted them, would be duly appreciated. In addition to the library of reference, the Institute should possess a museum, and a laboratory and

[33] In Mr. Henman's Lecture on Civil Engineering, and Machinery generally, he remarks, "In any industrial schools that may be established, I think it will be found that, for some time to come, so far as engineering is concerned, money will be better laid out in the library than the lecture-room; and indeed, with a few bright exceptions, we have not many men who possess the will and power to keep an audience constantly attentive on these subjects."

illustrative apparatus. No teaching is so effectual as *object teaching*, when the thinking powers are duly exercised; and if a principle or a fact of science is explained by an illustration palpable to the senses, the effect on the mind is then most vivid and lasting. Watch the interest with which numbers crowd round the platform at the conclusion of a popular scientific lecture. With what curiosity is each piece of apparatus examined! Such helps to instruction are as much required as are the models and drawings of the schools of design. What drawing is to the designer, the carver, and the trades requiring ornament, chemistry is to the dyer, bleacher, and calico-printer, and mechanics to the artizan employed in works of construction. Nothing could show more conclusively the utter disregard of what *should* be the primary object of these institutions than the fact, that in some of them there exist collections of valuable apparatus which have lain for years unused and covered with dust, as so much useless lumber; and this, too, in large seats of population and industry, where ample facilities exist for the formation of classes for the study of the different branches of science.

It should be borne in mind that those whom we wish to reach, have to perform a day's labour before they commence their studies. Considering the shortness of the time at their disposal, and that they are unaccustomed to habits of study, we see why every "appliance and means to boot" should be put within their reach, that the instruction may be as effective as possible while it lasts.

Whenever it is determined to put the educational machinery of our institutes on a proper footing, a system of examinations and certificates must be established. This would be preferable to giving occasional prizes, a plan which tends to breed ill-feeling among the pupils. Each class should have its separate certificate of the pupil having satisfactorily passed through a thorough examination. This is the plan followed in the Edinburgh School of Arts, wherein every pupil having satisfied the examiners as to his acquirements, acquires an "attestation of proficiency." If at the conclusion of three years' attendance the student can furnish attestations of proficiency in all the required studies, he receives a diploma of life-membership, certifying his knowledge on these studies, and giving him free admission to the lectures and library for life, on the payment of two shillings annually. Dr. Hudson justly observes, that "a certificate obtained by a course of study like this, and after examinations so searching and complete, is unquestionably one of the highest and most flattering testimonials which a young man can possess; it certifies at once the correctness of his conduct, the extent of his studies, and the proficiency he has made; and go where he will, and apply for what situation he may, this certificate of membership obtained so honourably, must ever be his best recommendation, as well as the most powerful stimulus to a line of conduct which should support the character he has acquired."

If the Industrial University in London becomes established, with its professorships, then might presentations be awarded to each institution embracing the requisite branches of instruction in its plan, and these would be conferred on those pupils who had gone creditably through their examinations, and whose merit and ability promised to repay any extra culture bestowed upon them. Having already stated the deficiencies of the lecturing system as now pursued, we simply suggest, that the remedy consists in diminishing, *not discontinuing entirely*, the number of miscellaneous lectures, and adding to each winter session, one or two complete courses on those branches of science, for which it was found impossible to provide regular class-instruction. In many places it would be difficult to establish classes for geology, physiology, astronomy, &c., however desirable a knowledge of their leading principles might be. But even here we would approximate the lectures to class-instruction, by enabling all who attended a complete course, and were willing to submit to an examination at the conclusion of the course, to do so, entitling those who passed it satisfactorily to honourable mention in the annual reports, or in the way that might be deemed best for the encouragement of the student. It is true, that no ordinary course of lectures, such as mechanics' institutes in their earlier, and in this respect better, days provided, could compare with the instruction received in the classes, but the student would have the opportunity, by means of the library, of filling up the chasms in his knowledge, as leisure and taste might dictate. It does not follow, because the acquisitions made by the working man cannot rival those of the professor, that they must therefore be useless. He may not become profound in any study, — who is versed in all? But he may learn many of the leading facts and principles of the most important departments of knowledge; and through the advancement of knowledge and the improved means of conveying it, any man of the least leisure may know more than did the greatest sages of antiquity. If little learning is a dangerous thing, less of it is more dangerous. Like a little money, or a little sense, it is useful as far as it goes.

There seems to us a good deal of mistake about what is called "first-class lectures." By all means let us have the best teaching and lecturing possible; but if only those lecturers are meant who are known to fame as the authors of great works, or great discoveries, we must demur to the recommendation; for if the people are to wait for instruction in science till they can have their lessons at the hands of a Faraday or a Brewster, they must wait for ever. What is wanted is, a correct and popular exposition of the subject; and though the lecturer should neither enter into all the minutiæ, nor even always state the several applications of the principles he communicates, nor have ever made a single discovery himself, he may yet be able to convey much and accurate knowledge to others. We have heard Dalton's atomic theory communicated to a popular audience in a better way than Dalton himself ever conveyed it. Indeed, no people's lecturer, whatever his eminence, attempts to give the refinements of his subject, because he knows the audience would not understand him if he did. Such disquisitions, fit enough at a meeting of *savans*, like the British Association, are out of place in a popular assembly.

There is one subject on which almost every advocate for increasing the efficiency of Mechanics' Institutes has proposed that they should offer instruction — viz., Political Economy. This subject, both from its own importance and the peculiar view we take of it, requires more than a passing remark. Dr. Chalmers, many years ago, recommended its introduction into Mechanics' Institutions.[34] If we differ from so great an authority, it is not because we underrate the importance of the subject, but because practical experience has shown that as yet opinion is too much divided, and party feeling too strong, to permit them to be discussed with calmness. The question as to the introduction of any subject, whether of religion, politics, or political economy, may be determined by the answer to this question: Is it intended to hear both sides? You only wish to diffuse *correct* views on important questions. Granted. But what is *correct?* Who is to be judge? Shall the Committee of the Institute, imitating larger conclaves, sit in judgment upon opinions, and decide by majority what is and what is not orthodox? Are we never to learn the lessons of history, which show that every opinion now boasting its majority was once in a minority — that

[34] Christian and Economic Polity of a Nation, chap. xxiv.

votes are worthless in matters of opinion? When the time comes, as assuredly it will, that truth shall be held more sacred than opinion, no one will object to free discussion. Common fairness,—the interests of Truth herself,—require that on every disputed topic, submitted to any body of men, they should be prepared to mete out the same fair condition to *both* sides of the question. Now, we believe the English mind has not yet reached this high standard; and it would therefore be impossible to unite any large support from men of all parties in behalf of an institution which *permitted* to all shades of thought the free expression of opinion. Such a union of all parties, however, is essential to any extensively beneficial operation, and therefore the next best thing is, *entire and strict neutrality* upon all those subjects whereon the fullest expression of opposite opinions would not be allowed.

However valuable lectures on political economy would be, therefore, the time has not yet arrived when they can be offered with advantage; because the spirit of party is still too violent to give all views a fair chance. Even if the Protectionist would allow the defence of free exchanges, the working man would feel that his view of the subject was not represented, often perhaps misrepresented, and he would stay away. No teacher in this country will gain the ear of the working-man, unless he is willing to have his opinions and statements canvassed, to invite the utterance of conflicting opinion, and to give to truth "a fair field, but no favour." This course has not been, and cannot be, adopted in mechanics' institutes, and, therefore, any attempt to convey economical doctrine, "sound or unsound," through their media must prove a failure. Those who deplore the fallacies entertained by the working-classes on the subjects of machinery, the poor-laws, etc. etc. must leave to other agencies the task of removing them.

The same objections do not apply to books as to lectures. Books, like newspapers, convince without exciting the heats of discussion, — are free from the triumphs of success, or the mortification of defeat. Impartiality in the selection is equally requisite as in the case of newspapers. Exclude, or include, *both sides* in fair proportions. Any other course manifests a doubt lest truth could take care of itself, and is a confusion of your individual right of opinion, with your *executive* power as a delegate for others.

Mechanics' institutes *need not*, however, be indifferent to questions affecting the social interests of the working-classes. That they *are* so is one great cause of their present inutility; but to their more intimate participation in those interests, we look for their power increasingly to attract the working-classes. Although the more debateable subjects cannot with safety be introduced, till a greater spirit of candour, forbearance, and kindness to opponents has grown up among us, there is a class of social questions of the highest importance to the working-man, and on which there is little difference of opinion. Lectures on sanitary regulations, in relation to ventilation, cleanliness, construction of dwellings, &c., would be of immense benefit to the community. Instruction on the importance of economising wages, and on the best kind of investments for the savings of the people, and popular lectures on the principles of assurance, are very much required. Large numbers of the people make no provision whatever for sickness, old age, and death, or those casualties to which all are liable. What is still more deplorable is, that the little provision usually made, is through the various descriptions of friendly societies, which are continually failing, owing to the false principles on which they are based. Much, indeed, might be done in this direction from the platform of the mechanics' institution, for the domestic and social improvement of the people, and for the originating of a higher public sentiment on many points connected with general and municipal legislation. We talk much of public opinion and its vast power, and, compared with some countries, have reasons to be proud of its achievements. But this public opinion is an effect even more than it is a cause. The thought inspires one or two men that slavery is wrong, and they proclaim this fact to the nation so loudly and so earnestly, that at last the nation listens, and we banish the accursed thing from our shores. A few men meeting in Newhall's Buildings, Manchester, declare, in a very prosaic way, that the corn-laws ought to be abolished. What *do* they? Send their lecturers from the Land's End to John o'Groats, scatter their tracts and essays by the million, and the corn-laws become a thing of history. Another set of men, perceiving that drink was the curse of the working-classes, determine to put it down, and tens of thousands of rescued and regenerated drunkards attest the victory of their lectures and their tracts.[35] The same instrumentality of free speech, and of a free press, is available to the friends of mechanics' institutions. It needs but men who know the value of such information to our people as they dispense, and have skill to organise the working-power, in order to effect more wonderful changes than any we have named. "How shall the people hear without a preacher? and how shall they preach, except they be sent?"

It is some compensation for the exclusion of economical along with other disputed topics, that astronomy or chemistry can in part subserve the same end. Dr. Chalmers has an eloquent passage that we will transcribe:—"Mechanic schools, even though the lessons of economic science should for ever be excluded from them,

[35] The *increase* in the consumption of intoxicating liquors, in the fifteen years previous to the commencement of the temperance agitation, was 50 per cent.; and in fifteen years succeeding, the *decrease* was 19 per cent.

are fitted to work the greatest of economic improvements in the condition of the people. Whatever may stimulate the powers of the understanding, or may regale the appetite for speculation, by even that glimmering and imperfect light which is made to play, in a mechanic school, among the mysteries of nature; or may unveil, though but partially, the great characteristics of wisdom and goodness that lie so profusely scattered over the face of visible things; or may both exalt and give a wider compass to the imagination; or may awaken a sense that before was dormant, to the beauties of Divine workmanship, and to the charms of that argument, or of that eloquence, by which they are expounded;—each and all of these might be pressed into the service of forming to ourselves a loftier population. Every hour that a workman can reclaim from the mere drudgeries of bone and muscle, will send him back to his workshop and his home a more erect and high-minded individual than before. With his growing affinity to the upper classes of life in mental cultivation, there will spring up an affinity of taste and habit, and a growing desire of enlargement from those various necessities by which the condition of a labourer may now be straitened and degraded."[36]

There are other methods than the direct communication of instruction, which may be beneficially adopted by Mechanics' Institutions. The scientific instruction of males and females takes the first place, in point of dignity and importance. If our institutes cannot offer it, they will be superseded by agencies that will. But scientific instruction is not alone important. As the artisan is not merely a *workman*, but a *man*, he should be, besides a skilful workman, a sober and well behaved citizen. We have stated how greatly general instruction is calculated to promote even this object, but it does not

[36] *Works*, vol. xvi., chap. xxiv.

exhaust all the methods that may be used to accomplish the desired end. Education is a broad term. Every act of life, every scene, every word uttered by oneself or others, leaves its impress upon character. Intelligent philanthropy, recognising the truth, has endeavoured to ameliorate the conditions of the workman's labour, and to improve the character of the workman's home. All honour to these efforts! None can be made that will prove richer in results. But Mechanics' Institutes claim no lower function; for they propose to *interest* "the leisure hour;" and what portion of life is of more importance, what more liable to abuse? They propose to carry forward the instruction which the infant school has but commenced, which the day school has but prepared for, to higher developments. And instruction in the sciences which have the most important bearing on a man's industrial pursuits, his domestic and his social economics, are not the only means of reaching them. Rational amusement and the presence of the beautiful, whether in nature or in art, all tend to close the avenues of his mind to baser pleasures, and to render him worthy of his human destiny.

In one of his addresses to the Manchester Mechanics' Institute [37], Sir Benjamin Heywood remarks:—"It was thought, and I joined in the opinion, that the study of physical science would essentially contribute to advancement, by its tendency to impress the mind with the infinite power, wisdom, and goodness which the Creator has displayed in all his works. I confess that, upon this point also, I have been disappointed; I do not find that 'to look through nature up to nature's God' is a necessary or even common accompaniment of the study of physical science; and I am anxious for an altered system of instruction, not merely that we may give to it more variety and interest, but that we may combine with it more moral improvement."

[37] October 11, 1832.

"What, then, is the modification of our plan which seems desirable? It is to adapt our instruction more to the taste and capacity of the working-classes, to make it more elementary and more entertaining, to extend it to a greater variety of subjects, and to connect with it more moral improvement."

Music, gymnastics, cricket, social tea-parties[38]; such seemed to be the proposed features of the recreative department.

Newspapers he did not approve of, but they were subsequently introduced. Very much controversy has existed as to whether institutions should embrace any other objects than those of direct elementary and scientific instruction, and many of their best friends have strongly opposed the introduction of much that has latterly formed part of their programme of attractions. Under suitable limitations, however, refining amusements, &c., may be introduced with advantage. It is urged that, by uniting newspapers, recreations, &c., with the strictly educational pursuits of the institution, that the force of the institution is diverted from essential to secondary matters, that there is fostered a taste for light pursuits, until at last people will take nothing solid, save where spiced with some attraction. Moreover, that however good these things may be in their due time and place, it is better to have a separate management and establishment for the various objects, than to agglomerate them into one.

There is force in these objections, but they are not decisive. To take the last point first; it is, doubtless, practicable in very large towns to separately establish many of the features combined with Mechanic's Institutions. There might be a society for providing recreation, another for furnishing cheap news-rooms,

38 The members even made a trip to Liverpool. Contrasted with our own monster trips of the present day, it seems odd to regard a party of "between thirty and forty" as an event.

another to take charge of the small savings of the youths[39], and so on. If each can be founded and supported on so large a scale as to render it possible to conduct them with equal economy of time and expense, if the town is so amply supplied with a public-spirited middle class for their management with vigour and high aims, there might perhaps be some advantage in a separate establishment. In the general run of towns, this state of things rarely prevails; in the villages, never. In most places few persons are able, and still fewer disposed, to devote their leisure to the management of societies for the public good; and the extent of the operations, when thus divided, would not allow of the employment of paid agents.

If the working-man must go to one place for his technical instruction, to another for his newspapers, to a third for his recreations, each would cost him more, and of each he would get less. But independently of such considerations, we think, an intrinsic advantage will be found in the combined plan; viz., that the *thirst for excitement* will be moderated in an institute where amusement takes both a subordinate and regulated place. How far such extraneous, but related objects shall be introduced, must be left to the good sense of the committee and subscribers. We presume only to offer a few observations on such features as seem capable of being introduced for good.

For a long time the introduction of newspapers was resisted as "inconsistent with the objects of the institution." The institutions lost many friends in the newspaper, as in every other contest; but they have always attracted additional members, so as to more than balance the loss. It is a real evil if the working-man has no opportunity to read both sides, and this is too much the case in the news-rooms dependent solely upon

[39] A special objection is made to the attaching of a savings bank to Mechanics' Institutes, viz: the *pecuniary responsibility* it involves.

the custom of the working-class. But in the mechanics' institute there is no favouritism in the selection. Indeed, no single instance of complaint on this ground has ever reached us. It is obviously of the highest importance that the working-man, anxious to read the newspapers, should not have to pay a beer or spirit tax to enjoy the privilege. Moreover, though newspapers do not convey the best or the highest knowledge, it is impossible to read them without acquiring both much information, and a habit of reasoning which is of great value in the affairs of life. Some people have a horror of pot-house politicians! With the exception of the pot-house part, we think every man should be a politician; and it will be ill for our country when its citizens shall delegate their interest in its welfare and affairs to others. The most rabid and radical cobbler that ever neglected his shoes to mend the state, is a better citizen than the cozy comfortable fellow, who would be a contented subject of the Grand Turk, if but secure of his dinner. "The difference," as Dr. Lees has remarked, "is not in the depreciated *subjective excitement*, but in the *objective* direction. The cultivated man or the half-read politician is *interested* in the political principle, the ignorant man *excited* by the political party. One works and reasons for measures, the other shouts and brawls for men."[40]

At the same time, we readily grant that newspaper reading may be carried to excess, and even abstract time that could be better employed in the classes. The Duke of Argyll thus eloquently deprecates *too much* newspaper reading:—"If you wish to be living always in the present,—if you wish to have the din of its contentions always in your ears, and the flush of its fleeting interests for ever on your brow,—above all, if you wish to have your opinions ready-made for you without

[40] *Truth Seeker*, 1845.

the trouble of inquiry, and without the discipline of thought,—then, I say, come from your counting-house and spend the few hours of leisure which you may have, in exhausting the columns of the daily press; but if your ambition be a nobler one,—if your aim be higher, you will find yourselves often passing from the door of the news-room into that of the library,—from the present to the past,—from the living to the dead,—to commune with those thoughts which have stood the test of time, and which have been raised to the shelves of the library by the common consent of all men, because they do not contain mere floating information, but instruction for all generations and for all time."

The evil might be greatly obviated by admitting no person to the news-room under twenty-five years of age, and by making the fee of admission to include all the other departments of the institute. In some institutes a separate fee has been charged for the news-room, which only helps to exclude the poorer members and attract those whose circumstances do not require a cheap news-room.

Nor can we go with those who would exclude moderate and rational amusement from the province of our Mechanics' Institutes. It need not interfere much with other duties of the managers, to provide an occasional concert or a dramatic reading. On the other hand, leave the entire amusement of the working-man to be provided by private enterprise, and it will be found that those who cater to popular wants for gain, must adapt their treat to the low tastes of those who pay for it. It is no longer a question of social morals, but of supply and demand; not of the elevation of the popular taste, but of gratification. Have the objectors considered the alternative? Have they ever visited our singing-rooms and casinos? It is not drink, much as our people are given to drinking, which attracts the majority of the people there. The casino supplies what neither the gin-palace, nor the beer-house supplies —amusement; a transient relief from the exhaustion and monotony of daily toil. We have ourselves counted 1300 young men and women in one such place at one time.[41] *There* the young man learns to smoke and drink, and the sooner he does so, he fancies, the better he asserts his manliness. *There* the young female learns the meaning of coarse and indelicate allusions, and what is worse, to laugh at them, the descent to prostitution is afterwards neither difficult nor slow. *There* the grossest buffoonery may be heard, and the stupidest exhibition seen. What sort of school is this, whence to expect good servants or dutiful children?—what sort of preparation is it for those who either already have assumed, or shortly will assume the responsibilities of married life,—of parental obligation? How will they become fitted to be the manly citizens of a free country? These are questions which the legislator, the patriot, and all who have any interest in our country's well-being, would do well to consider. And let us not blame the working-classes, at least not solely. Few of them had ever an opportunity of knowing better. If they went to school at all, they were removed before they could be permantly impressed. They have seldom cheerful homes, supplied with the attractions and comforts of life. Would the young man enjoy the charms of music? There are no nimble ready fingers to touch the piano; no fine books, engravings, or chess-board to wile away a spare hour. Fatigued with the day's toil what shall he do for a little excitement, or how ward off sleep till bedtime? Exclude the working-man from opportunities of spending a leisure hour unprofitably if you like, and you shut the door of your institute on half of those who now enjoy its advantages. To raise the working-man we must take hold of him where he is, not

[41] See Appendix C.

where he is not. Attract him, get possession of him, and you may lead him by degrees to something better. Those who are students will, when suitable teachers are obtained, find their congenial employment—those who are not, will at least find harmless ways of spending time. Minerva, with a stern aspect, should never be the emblem of a people's institute; rather let us take radiant Apollo, who bears his harp as companion to his philosophy.

In small villages, the attractions of the institute, like its instructions, cannot be so complete and perfect in their character as in large towns. The Hon. and Rev. Sydney Godolphin Osborne, who looks at these topics as practical questions to be dealt with, proposes that there should be a sort of *moral beer-house* opened in these villages, where the meal of bread and cheese and beer, and even the pipe, should not be excluded. In a large well lighted, well warmed, convenient room, under the control of a steward, one of the more respectable inhabitants of the village, he would provide "a small bookcase, under the steward's custody; in this, for the use of the members, we would keep a certain number of plain amusing books, chiefly of a secular character. From time to time, these books to be changed for others of a like nature. On the same tables we would place copies of such works as the 'Illustrated News' perhaps a number or two of the county or other newspapers." The steward should have no interest in the sale of the beer, of which only a limited quantity should be admitted. Spirits, gambling, quarrelling or bad language not to be allowed and no person under eighteen to be admitted. As an experiment where a higher order of institute is impracticable, and where habits of drunkenness have taken hold of the population, the suggestion deserves a trial. By degrees a few more books, a few more classes, and now and then an interesting lecture; and no doubt the members of the *moral beer-house* would themselves speedily vote the expulsion of John Barleycorn and his smoking companion.[42] Speaking of the Miles Platting Institution, Sir. B. Heywood, in one of his addresses at the Manchester Institution, said "We are endeavouring to make our reading-room there very popular, to have in an evening a blazing fire, red curtains, easy chairs, a capital cup of coffee, chess, pictures, now and then a good story read aloud, now and then a good song; in short, to see if we cannot make it a match for the public house, as a place of resort for the working-man after his day's work. In summer we should be glad to see conveniences for gymnastics, cricket, and other manly exercises; and it would add many years to life, especially to those engaged in sedentary occupations, as clerks, tailors, shoemakers, &c. At some institutions they have been introduced with great advantage. Gymnastic exercises in the Manchester Mechanics' Institute materially improved the health of the members. A swimming-bath would be a useful addition. In winter, meetings of a social character should be encouraged."

Another very advantageous way of refining the taste, and increasing the information of the working-classes, is by occasional exhibitions. When well managed, they materially improve the finances of the institution. The exhibitions, as they have been usually held in connection with mechanics' institutes, are a sort of polytechnic gallery of works of art, as pictures and statues, models of machinery, specimens of natural productions, &c. Most of the objects are lent by persons in the town and

42 The public-houses have made some advance; for the number of newspapers has been greatly increased, and in some instances nights have been set apart for political discussions, which have been well sustained in the bar-parlours. At an inn in the Kennington Road, lectures on Astronomy have been delivered to extensive smokers, before whom were the ale-pots and the alcoholic mixtures. In several of the suburban districts a few books have been introduced into the public-houses, for the use of parlour visitors; and there is an indication of improvement springing up which may commend the future.—*Hist. of Adult Education*, p. 211.

its neighbourhood, but a few are hired. To a man of benevolent mind the gratification derived from a beautiful work of art which he may possess, is doubled by participation. And that pleasure must be heightened by the reflection that he is rendering most important aid to the funds of the institution. If the gain to the person who spares a picture from his drawing-room, a statue from his hall, or a machine from his shop, is great; if the funds of the institute are increased, and the attention of large classes attracted to the advantages of an institute whose very existence was unknown to them,—the gain to the public is no less. At an almost nominal sum the inhabitants of a small town are enabled to view a collection of objects whose cost and extent would not be unworthy of the metropolis itself.

The first exhibition of this character was that of the Manchester Mechanics' Institute; it was opened on the 27th of December, 1837, and remained open nearly six weeks, and was visited by upwards of 50,000 persons. Speaking of it at the following annual meeting of the members[43], Sir Benjamin Heywood, in the warmth of his feelings said:—"How delightful is the contemplation of everything connected with it! Where shall I begin in the enumeration of its happy influences? Shall I speak of the spirit which animated those who undertook its preparation and arrangement, of the days and nights of labour they devoted to it; of the readiness and kindness with which contributions of all kinds were offered to it by thousands and tens of thousands, who had never seen anything of the kind before; of the new and nobler taste which it has awakened in the minds of many of them? or shall I speak of its value as an example to other institutions, possessing rich and beautiful collections, from which the public have hitherto been excluded? It was delightful to see the countenances, beaming with pleasure, of the working men,

[43] Feb. 28th, 1838.

their wives, and their children, as they thronged through the rooms, and gazed upon different objects; and I could not help feeling in how many of their breasts a chord must have been touched, the vibration of which will have given life and permanence to new and happier feelings within them. I could not help feeling, when I saw every article of the exhibition exposed before them, and immediately within their reach, and learned that the exhibition closed without injury to a single specimen, how false an estimate those have formed, who dare not trust their collections to public inspection. Surely the example will not be lost. Oh! let it be known throughout the country, let it open doors that have hitherto been closed, let our own town be the first to profit by the example, and let us see our National History Society, our Royal Institution, our Botanic Garden, our Zoological Garden thronged, as your exhibition has been with working-men and their families. Treat the working-man with generosity and confidence, and he will repay you with honesty and gratitude; treat him with suspicion and distrust, and what right have you to expect a different return?"

So successful a beginning was sure to be imitated. At Sheffield, Ripon, Gateshead, public exhibitions were got up.[44] The Liverpool Mechanics' Institute has had three exhibitions. By the first, in 1840, they cleared 2093*l.*; by the second, in 1842, 2000*l.*; and by that in 1844, 1100*l.*; or a total of 5200*l.*, and this, notwithstanding many thousands of children, and the police, and military, were admitted free. In Leeds, an exhibition was held in 1839, and the results were equally gratifying. The report of the directors thus speaks of it:—"Deep regret was expressed, again and again, that either that, or some similar place of resort, could not be kept open throughout a large portion of the

[44] See Appendix D.

year, by many whose previous resort had been to places of low gratification, or who had listlessly whiled away their time in mere idleness. The committee feel every assurance that much good was done by the experiment. Their space will not allow of enlargement; but they may enumerate the following as the most important and valuable results:—kindness and liberality in meeting and gratifying the public taste, by the more wealthy members of society, were largely elicited; public spirit was developed in the arduous performance of most onerous duties, and largely encouraged and rewarded by the success attendant on their faithful discharge; it was demonstrated that other gratifications than the grosser ones of the appetite have power over a large portion of the community, and the public at large may be safely admitted to the inspection of the most valuable collections of art and nature; it was further shown that sentiments of kindliness, and habits of courtesy and order, are more generally spread throughout society than is commonly believed; and lastly, the wonders of human art, and the works of the Deity, miracles compared with those wonders—were brought before the close gaze of nearly a hundred thousand persons, the greater proportion of which immense number had never before enjoyed such a spectacle; and it cannot be doubted that a great stimulus has thereby been given to a laudable curiosity, to scientific inquiry, and generally to the cultivation of such tastes and habits as must materially aid the moral progress of society."[45]

[45] The attendance of visitors, and the pecuniary results were as under, the exhibition being open three months.

	£	s.	d.
87,908 persons were admitted at 6*d*. each. - -	2197	14	0
6220 were admitted by Season Tickets, at 2*s*. 6*d*. -	777	10	0
Sale of Catalogue, Poetry printed at the Exhibition, Confectionary, &c. - - - - - - -	425	0	0
Total.	3400	4	0

Permanent exhibitions of the *same objects* would soon lose their novelty and attractiveness, and consequently their chief value. In our large towns annual or biennal exhibitions, on the same plan as those of the Mechanics' Institutes in the United States, would be very useful. These Institutes, says Dr. Hudson, "hold annual fairs for the exhibition of mechanical arts, and any person has the privilege of depositing machinery or manufactured goods of any description, or the raw material. These exhibitions or fairs generally last two or three weeks, and are profitable not only to the Institution, but to persons exhibiting machinery or goods."[46] Speaking of the Institutes in our Canadian possessions, he remarks, "their annual exhibitions are purely of a practical nature, affording the best popular evidence of the progress of scientific discovery. The managers of the Canadian Mechanics' Institutions endeavour to instil into the minds of their members a regard for the great principles of the Arts; and they serve to impress upon the thousands who visit thier exhibitions, the importance of the study of physical science, as the chief element in the development of civilisation. Their exhibitions extend beyond the Polytechnic exhibitions of London; for while they elucidate, by short lectures, the value and importance of new discoveries in science, the best methods of farming, and point out the desirability of creating as it were new articles in produce, they carefully abstain from the fire cloud and phantasmagoria, and apportion their receipts to the extension of the library, and the improvement of the mechanical workshops."

"The total number of visits paid by the holders of Season Tickets was 96,005, forming, with the single admissions of 87,908 persons, a total number of visits of 183,913. The expenses were of course considerable, amounting to upwards of 1600*l.*, yet leaving a balance of 1800*l.*, with which the committee, aided by a further subscription from several spirited individuals, have purchased a very suitable Hall for the Institute."—*Leeds Report*, 1840.

[46] History of Adult Education, pp. 218 and 219.

Excursions have been frequently made by the members of Mechanics' Institutes, to places memorable for their beauty or their historic associations. In the present day, when excursions are so plentifully offered by the railway companies or parties contracting with them, committees need scarcely divert their energies from the general purposes to provide them. If the excursion were combined with some interesting account of the locality visited, *on the spot*, such visits would have a highly educational value, might occasionally be conducted by the Institutes, and when done judiciously, would render pecuniary aid to its funds. The Saturday half-holidays, now becoming general, would afford fine opportunities for short excursions, pedestrian or otherwise, and under the direction of an intelligent member of the Institute, might be useful in the study of nature, the natural history of the district, and the formation of local museums.

One very advantageous feature has been added to a few Institutes in Yorkshire, for the purpose of fostering and forming more economical habits among the youths of these Institutes. We allude to the Penny Savings' Banks proposed in 1850, by Mr. Charles W. Sykes, of Huddersfield. His plan is briefly as follows: —

"I venture to suggest a method hitherto untried, namely, that the humbler members of each Mechanics' Institution should be encouraged to 'transact a little business, with a preliminary savings' bank within the Institution, for which purpose some of the leading members might form a small 'Savings' Bank Committee,' attending an evening weekly to receive their trifling deposits — their threepences — their sixpences, and, perhaps, their shillings — giving each party a small book, and so on as his sum reached, say 2*l.* 2*s.*, paying it over to the Government savings' bank of the town, in the person's name, and giving to him or her the new pass-book. This is to be repeated until another guinea be accumulated, to be again transferred, and so on,—no interest being allowed until paid over to the Government savings' bank. The little book-keeping requisite would be very simple—and from always being paid over when it reached 1*l.* 1*s.*, or 2*l.* 2*s.*, the liability incurred would be very limited. A list of the balances (with the ledger folio corresponding with the pass-book, and signed by the treasurer) to be suspended in the room each half year, thus enabling each depositor to see that his money is safe." The plan has been adopted in several Institutes with great success. The humble savings here commenced will doubtless, in numerous instances, form a foundation for habits of prudence and economy. It is certain that much money thus saved will find its way to the funds of the Institution itself, or promote objects of an equally beneficial character. Although it would be undesirable, and perhaps impracticable, for Mechanics' Institutes to mix themselves up with the practical conducting of the affairs of Friendly and similar Societies, they might benefit both those societies and themselves by providing accommodation for their meetings. The working man visiting his club would oftener stray into the reading room or the library, than, as he now does, into the tap room or the bar. The heavy tax now levied "for the good of the house," would be directed into the fund of the Society or of the Institute, for his own benefit instead of the publican's.

Another way of inducing the working classes to feel a more intimate connexion between such Institutions and their material well-being, would be by providing proper means for registering the names of employers seeking workmen, and of workmen seeking employment. If the register for the latter specified the classes in which the workmen had attained proficiency, employers seeking for a man of superior qualifications would know where to look for him. The registers of the local Institutes might be sent to a central union of Institutes, and there be classified and arranged under the heads of the respective trades. It should then be printed and returned to the respective societies, and thus the working man in search of employment would learn not only the name of employers in his own locality seeking his services, but those of employers all over the kingdom, a matter to him of immense importance now that railways have so facilitated intercourse. He might thereby often be saved long months of privation, idleness, and its consequent bad habits, or avoid an inroad upon the little store saved up against the season of sickness and age. The machinery required for such a plan is obviously so very simple, consisting merely of a properly kept register, open for reference to all, whether employers or employed, connected with the Institute, that we make no apology for proposing it. We are convinced, that if efficiently carried out, few plans would more tend to attract both these classes to support the Institute in return for the valuable assistance thus rendered.

A general remark may be added as to the introduction of amusement or objects of a still more important nature, namely, that they must ever be subordinate to the main purposes of the Institute, which should never be permitted to degenerate into a mere news-room, or a club for concerts and dramatic readings. We do not, as we have said, consider such things generally incompatible with rigorous attention to the class and lecture instruction, but in some circumstances they may become so—and, in such instances, we had better omit amusement entirely, than peril the efficiency of these important departments.

CHAPTER III.

BUSINESS MANAGEMENT.

We have stated as briefly as the subject admits of, some of the deficiencies of Mechanics' and similar Institutes, and endeavoured to point out those which it is peculiarly desirable should be supplied. Between those social reforms to be desired, and those that can be achieved, there is in a popularly governed society like our own a great gulf fixed. "So many men, so many minds," is here the rule. In this country every department of our great national institutions is the result of growth from small beginnings, sometimes of centuries. We do not adopt schemes of improvement suddenly and entire, however desirable the end. So it will be with Adult Education. It would be easy to propose grand schemes of instruction, borrowed from the American or continental models, highly excellent in themselves. But when we are so far in the wake even in the primary instruction of the day school, it is vain to expect that we shall at once recover our way in adult instruction. No proposal will be listened to which does not go upon the basis of existing agencies. Little as some may estimate the Mechanics' Institutes, they may not be superseded. Whatever interest the people have in their own education, is centered there. They embrace those who best love popular improvement, who have devoted the energies of their life to this work — men who bore the standard of progress during the burden and heat of the day of opposition and of conflict.

The first step required to render these Institutes adequate to the purposes aimed at, is *to increase the means at their disposal.* Unless this is done, we see little chance of their improvement. There are three sources from which such an increase may be derived:

1st. The contribution of the working classes themselves;

2nd. The donations of the wealthy; and,

3rd. Aid from the State.

That the working classes do not contribute enough to pay for any adequate instruction is well known. There is some excuse for this in the fact, that since the year 1823, when these Institutes were first established, up to the last two years, their condition has generally been most depressed. Gleams of prosperity there have been, but the working man had scarcely begun to bask therein, when over-trading, bubble speculations, bad harvests, produced a commercial crisis, and consequent wide-spread privation. Making all reasonable deductions for such circumstances, we are of opinion, contrary to the prevalent impression, that the rate of contribution has been fixed too low. The object was to meet the working man's small resources, but the consequence has been the establishment of a vicious precedent, whose influence it will be difficult to abolish. From facts we have ascertained, it appears that out of 100 Institutes there were 18 Institutes in which the average annual subscription was under 5*s.*

51	Institutes above	5*s.*	and under	10*s.*
21	„	10*s.*	„	12*s.*
11	„	12*s.*	„	20*s.*[46a]

The total income of 103 Institutes in the Yorkshire Union, was in 1852, 8452*l.* or an average of about 82*l.* per Institute.[47] This is a very small sum to main-

[46a] Out of 13,000 members in eighty-one Institutes in Yorkshire, whose subscriptions were classified, upwards of 8000 members pay a sum under 2*d.* per week, and 6000 or nearly half, pay under 1½*d.* per week. — *Yorkshire Union Report*, 1853.

[47] In 1840, returns from ninety-six Institutes in all parts of the country showed a total income of 8356*l.*, or an average of 87*l.* per Institute; and in the same year, returns from seventy-nine Institutes showed that the average *minimum* rate of contribution was 4*s.* 6*d.* per year, and the average *maximum* rate 14*s.*

tain even a small Institute efficiently. Deduct rent, gas, fire, expense of books, periodicals and papers, binding, cleaning, attendance of managers and secretaries, and what is there left for the payment of lectures and teachers? A difference necessarily exists between Institutes in the towns and those in the rural districts, owing to the difference of wages. But no principle of relation between the cost of the thing wanted and the price charge for it, has ever been attempted to be ascertained. In one little village where the management of the Institute happens to be good, as much as 13*s.* per head per annum is contributed, while scores of Institutes with from twice to ten times the populations, hobble on with about 1*d.* per week, or 4*s.* per annum from each member. Now either one charge is too high or the other is too low, and those who have had the practical management of Institutions will not hesitate to affirm the latter alternative. To think that a sum not more than what the working man is willing to pay to a barber for shaving his beard, or to a publican for a single glass of beer, is to be charged for all the advantages which such an Institute professes to afford,—library, news-room, classes, lectures—a week's education and amusement,—is preposterous. We are acquainted with an Institution, in a busy manufacturing town containing 10,000 inhabitants, where the total income for paying rent, lighting, cleaning, attendance, lectures, teachers, books, and periodicals, is not above 25*l.* per annum! A sum which the keeper of any of its "free and easy" singing saloons would consider a small sum for providing the liquor and amusement of a single week. With such ridiculously small incomes, the committees of these Institutions can provide no advantages to tempt the working man within the walls. If he wants a clean, comfortable, well lighted and well warmed room, he is much more likely to find it at the ale-house, than at the Institution. If he wants teaching, he soon discovers that here at least nothing can be taught that can interest or improve him. He does not subscribe to the Institute, for he can gain nothing by so doing, and the Institute can give nothing because he furnishes no means,—thus an unfortunate circle, in which small means and small advantages mutually alternate as cause and effect, is established. In the present uninstructed condition of the working classes, there is but small hope that the remedy for this state of things will be initiated by them,—but could ample facilities and advantages be furnished to them by any means in the first instance, there is no doubt that much larger members would join these Institutions, so that a considerably higher but not excessive rate of subscription might be obtained from them, probably double or even treble the amount now paid.

Experience indicates that the amount obtainable from the working classes might be much increased by taking it in small sums. A pound per year, paid weekly, or at short intervals, would be far less formidable than paid at yearly or half-yearly periods, though both modes of payment should be adopted.[48]

Another source from which increased funds might possibly be looked for, is the contributions of the wealthy. We say possibly, for unless some increased inducement were held out to that class, much more could not be obtained from them. If they saw that superior workmen were produced by better instruction being afforded, they would do more. There are many who object to any contributions to these Institutes from the richer classes. They urge that these Institutions "*ought* to be self-supporting." Since the improved prospects of trade and increased demand for labour have given general employment, and to some extent raised wages, many who did contribute have withheld or di-

[48] In the Huddersfield Institute the payments are fortnightly.

minished their help under the plea. From one point of view the proposition seems reasonable enough. They who enjoy an advantage ought to pay for it. Moreover, looking at the fifty millions spent in intoxicating liquors, and the additional six or seven millions in tobacco, to say nothing of other equally objectionable expenditure, no one can doubt that the working classes *can* pay for their education. But these considerations do not decide the question. When they are urged as honest objections, and not merely as an excuse to avoid giving (for to this class of objectors no reply would be conclusive), it is forgotten that they imply in the working classes the possession of the very qualities whose absence is deplored. Men *ought* to be virtuous, religious, &c. &c.; but no sane man thinks that in having uttered these truisms he supersedes an obligation resting on him and on all to seek the realisation of such conditions where they do not exist. We might as well refuse our contribution to the Missionary Fund, "because the Blacks ought to evangelize themselves," as refuse aid to Mechanics' Institutes, because they ought to be self-supporting. When the savage *is* converted, he will support his own church, so when the working-man *is* educated, he will support his own college; and to this standard we should endeavour to attain. Nor does the obligation to contribute to the elevation of one's fellow creatures terminate by giving a pecuniary subscription. Help given in such a way as to destroy habits of self-dependence is ever mischievous. Contributions from the wealthy may be so appropriated as merely to reduce the subscriptions of the members. The working-men, instead of paying 4*d.* or 6*d.* a week, pays 2*d.* or 1*d.* The utility of the Institute is not increased a whit, the subscription is reduced till it bears no proportion to the income of the working man, or to his expenditure on objects of infinitely less value and importance. The cheapness is false, because the quality of the article is bad; the charity is false, because it cripples, while it professes to support. We could name Institutions which regard the funds supplied by those who never enter their walls as the regular means of support, and the contributions of the members as accidental and uncertain! The true principle is for the working man to contribute at the highest rate he can fairly afford; and as this may not provide means of instruction so good as is to be desired, let whatever aid he receives go to increase its *effectiveness*, — in short, give him a *better* article for the *same* money, rather than a *worse* article at *less*.

That the working classes will pay a much larger sum than is usually asked from them by these Institutes, is shown by the fact, that they paid 6*d*. per week, and 1*s*. per quarter in addition, to the People's College at Sheffield, a rate higher than is paid to any similar Institute in the country. Of course they will not pay the price of a good article, if only an inferior one is offered to them.

With this proviso, we scarcely know of any better means which the wealthy can adopt for benefiting themselves, for securing the affections of those around them, and to abolish a multitude of costly but *mischievous* charities, than supporting these Institutes. The excellent Lord Carlisle, then Lord Morpeth, in his address to the Manchester Mechanics' Institute[49], in appealing for help to the wealthy says, "living as they do in the midst of a dense and teeming population, I am thoroughly persuaded that the best and easiest method which they can adopt for obviating the risks necessarily incidental to such a state of society, is by diffusing, to the furthest extent of their means, that sound and useful knowledge which is not only a source of independent occupation and gratification in itself, but

[49] January 14. 1834.

which also imparts those principles in which are ever to be found the safest guides for individual conduct and the guarantees of public order." He asks of those "who enjoy all the resources and recreations of knowledge, whether they do not owe it to those who, by their patient and persevering industry, form the real basis of our collective wealth, and the real sinews of our national strength, to open as freely and widely as they can, those sources of blameless pleasure and wholesome improvement, 'which cheer but not inebriate,' and that general field of intellectual cultivation in which there is no exclusive right or prescriptive privilege, but which returns to all who till its gracious soil the most wholesome nourishment that can invigorate, refine, and elevate our common nature." We yet want in behalf of the people's colleges of to-day, something of that large generosity which endowed our grammar schools and colleges of past times. We inherit their gifts; shame to us, if with our larger means and still larger professions, we do not transmit similar blessings!

Some people say, throw overboard this system of patronage; try to do without the attraction of having a live lord to draw people to your *soirées*, and let these Institutions stand on their own merits. With all our heart, if it can be done; but any one who knows either the genius of the English people, or the difficulties with which these Institutes are still encumbered, will not use this language. Our countrymen respect rank and wealth, and when these are the accessories to splendid talents and great virtues they are right in so doing. Moreover a large number of persons look at rather who supports an object, than at the object itself. And as Mechanics' Institutions were at first impeded by a host of groundless suspicions, and even in some quarters are still dreaded as nests of revolution, nurseries for schism and infidelity, as places where poor people learn to be discontented with their position, &c., the only way of guiding this unthinking crowd, is for men whose standing and opinion even *they* must treat with respect, to show that they hold such objections as worthless, by themselves aiding such Institutes with their purses, and by taking part in their public proceedings. When a Carlisle, or a Russell, a Newcastle, or an Argyle, visits such Institutions, it is no " snobishness" (to use a vulgarism) that sees therein a value far outweighing the trifling inconvenience they incur. Certain people who read little and reason less, and who assuredly never take up with a new opinion, if its acquisition costs any trouble, are led to withdraw their hostility, even if they are not carried on so far as to aid these Institutions. We have not too much patronage, but too little, and we should not rest contented till we have the highest in the land, not merely with the empty parade of a name, but the same active participation which so materially crowned with success the results of the Great Exhibition.

And while we are speaking of patronage to these Institutions, we may perhaps refer to the position which the clergy sustains to them. It is a matter to be deeply regretted that the clergy have not taken an active part in aiding and promoting them. The consequence of the clergy holding aloof is bad in the towns, as it gives the Institutions a sectional and party character foreign to their design and nature. But in the rural districts, the opposition, tacit or avowed, of the clergy, where it prevails far too generally, either prevents such an Institution existing at all, or destroys its efficiency. In villages, the pastor generally controls the use of the school-room, the only decent room available for meetings. His sanction, or his disapproval, makes all the difference between its being fashionable, or the reverse, to support and visit the Institution. He is often the only man in the place whose education would enable him to transact the business, or guide to useful purpose the details of the Institution. Even when disposed to aid the Institution, it is often rather in the capacity of self-elected dictator than in that of its director and friend. His very position would always secure him all the real influence he could justly desire; but he frequently loses it all, and breaks up the Institute for want of a little tact and management. Drunkenness, sensuality, the most utter ignorance of every argument, and even of the very language, which week by week he addresses to the people, prevail, and he throws away, as of no worth, one of the strongest supports he could have. In failing to identify himself with the Institute he shuts himself out of one of the best channels for reaching the intellects and the hearts of his parishioners. It is to be hoped that the example of Archbishop Whately, of the Bishop of St. David's, the Dean of Ripon, and the advice of Dr. Hook [50], as to co-operation in carrying out the objects of these Institutes, will do much to change the opposition, or at least coldness, of the village clergy towards them.

Assuming the largest practicable contributions on the part of the working classes, and aided by still larger help on the part of the wealthy, we do not think that the claims of Adult Education can even then be adequately met. Institutions whose members consist of the middle class, and which chiefly offer the attractions of the circulating library, concerts, miscellaneous lectures and dramatic readings, *may*, if well managed, be self-supporting. But institutions meant to teach mainly the operative classes, and offer good elementary training, like the Huddersfield Institute, or scientific instructions like the Edinburgh School of Arts, cannot be self-supporting *now*, whatever they may ultimately become. The Huddersfield Institute's income last year was 650*l.*, of which sum 143*l.* was derived from persons who do not directly participate in the benefits of the institution,

[50] Lecture on Adult Education.

and 507*l.* from the fees of the pupil. The average annual fees from the Edinburgh School of Arts do not amount to above *half the actual expenditure*, the rest being contributed by the wealthy inhabitants of the city, without which, say the directors, "it could not be carried on a single session."[51] If this is the case with only the ordinary expenditure, how much more is it so with the first outfit and establishment of such Institutes. The funds with which the School of Arts was at first established were mainly furnished by the wealthy, and they did not allow the members the slightest control in its management. As frequently happens, the subscribers got tired of subscribing, and an application was made to Government for assistance, which proved unsuccessful.[52] And if in "Modern Athens" the payments of the members, and the liberal subscription of the wealthy, will not provide adequate means, where else in the Empire shall we find city or town from which we can expect to obtain a larger amount of support? Self-supporting in the proper sense of the word these Institutes are not, they are all assisted, to a considerable extent, by those who derive no direct benefit from them. The only question is, whether they shall receive adequate support or not,—a support not dependent on whim, caprice, or prejudices, but on the perception of their merits, and therefore a support to be relied upon. Competent teachers and lecturers, and secretaries, and managers, properly remunerated for their services; museums, laboratories, and libraries of the higher class of scientific and artistic works, are poorly furnished in the best supported Institutes, and not at all in the ill supported, which are the vast majority. The whole system is one of make-shift, and unless some more powerful

[51] History of Adult Education, p. 77.

[52] *Fortunately*, says Dr. Hudson, *unfortunately* we think, not only for the interests of the School of Arts, but for those of adult education in the country at large. Dr. Hudson objects to assistance from the State. We have carefully examined his valuable work to find the premises on which his objections rest — but in vain.

agency be introduced seems likely to remain so. Make-shift building, make-shift lectures, make-shift teachers, make-shift books, serve for want of better; in fact, a sort of *best-we-can-get* principle is adopted. And as a natural consequence the building costs much money in alterations, which had it been constructed for the purpose would never have been needed. The lectures are sometimes good, but oftentimes inferior. The teachers, unable to give more than the fag-end of their time, do not give even that very punctually. And the books, which are sometimes cast-aways from the rich man's library, are seldom of a character to interest the frequenters of the Institute. For these results, so deplorable when we look at the mighty interests moral and social involved, the conductors of these Institutions are in no degree responsible. Poor men, as many of them are, or, if well to do, often taxed very disproportionately to their means for benevolent objects, they cannot undertake to provide the requisite building and other means. All honour to them for what they do already, honour too to those who devote hours taken from their little leisure, and even from sleep, to the preparation of lectures in such Institutes; but, above all, honour to those who, after their day's toil is over, begrudge not in the hour or two left them, the labour of imparting their humble stock of knowledge to those less instructed than themselves. We have seen many a time the sacrifice and self-devotion of these humble labourers in the cause of social progress. Compared with theirs, how small the annual sacrifice, if indeed it be worth the name, of a few pounds on the part of the man of wealth. But this lamentable state of things shows that some stronger power must be brought to bear, and this leads us to consider the third source to which we must look for help, viz., a contribution from the State. It will serve to remove many objections that will at once be raised at the very sound of such a proposal, if we state *in limine* the nature of the assistance which seems advisable.

There is a very clear and obvious distinction between the systematic instruction in the principles of those arts and sciences which have a great industrial and social importance, wherein our Institutions are most deficient, and those pursuits that possess more of a personal interest, and which the Institutes have best succeeded in providing. It is on the former ground that the Institutes lay claim to whatever aid they can get from the outside public; on the latter that they principally obtain the support of their own members. Efficient class instruction in the arts and sciences, and the providing of all appliances requisite to make that instruction effective, the State should provide where deficient.

They come under that class of objects which, while universally recognised as of the highest value, will not be self-originating, scarcely even self-supporting when originated. They can no more be tried by commercial principles than can our British Museum, the National Gallery, or the defences of the country. The means of the scientific instruction of the people, if not entirely, yet in no small degree, must be supplied by the Government, until it is sufficiently perfected and appreciated by the mass of the community to be provided by themselves. Education of the character we refer to is intimately bound up with the future welfare and prosperity of this country.

On the other hand, there is a class of objects embraced by these Institutions, which, though not without their social value, are principally of interest to the individual partaking of them, and what is more to the point, which he is very likely to provide for himself. In this department we should include that portion of the library devoted to works of imagination and the lighter class of literature, lectures on miscellaneous subjects, amusements, and even those studies which come under the category of the luxuries of knowledge rather than its essentials. These may be trusted to the ordinary principle of supply and demand. Even apart from Mechanics' Institutes, the news-room, the novel-circulating library, and the concert, pay as commercial speculations. It is not meant to relieve the working-man from payment for such objects. But if he were relieved in part of the heavy payment requisite to provide essentially good instruction, he would be able to afford all that is otherwise requisite.

We are aware of the opposition which any proposal of aid from Government to Mechanics' Institutes will awaken among some of their warmest supporters. On the other hand, if the aid were coupled with no objectionable conditions, we believe the majority would be gladly prepared to avail themselves of it. Before speaking of the method in which Government might best afford assistance to Mechanics' Institutes, we will glance at one or two objections sometimes urged against such aid. There is no need to discuss here the question of the right of the Government interference, since public opinion already sanctions all that the Government has done, and loudly calls upon it to do much more. So long as we exact obedience to the laws, and cause Government to punish their infraction, we are bound to qualify the governed to obey those laws. The right to education is but the inference from the duty of obedience.

The principle of leaving education entirely to the ordinary commercial principles of "supply and demand," cannot logically be maintained by those who think the subscriptions of the wealthy desirable as aids to Mechanics' Institutes. The ground on which they must appeal for help is that the poor have not means to obtain all the education for themselves which it is desirable, on public grounds, that they should possess. No other plea for assistance is tenable. Demand, in the commercial sense, as implying the desire and the means of obtaining instruction, does not exist, at least to any adequate extent. The ignorant do not value education, and, if it were offered, would not be able to judge of its merits for themselves. The same principle cannot then be applied to education as to loaves of bread or cotton gowns. But society has the deepest interest that the means of education should be plentifully provided, and that as many as possible should partake of its advantages. Of no other commodity can this be so emphatically said as of instruction. In the case of adults, we do not of course believe that education should be compulsory. There is a very long interval between affording facilities and encouragements to an object, and the taking a step which would be as impossible as it is undesirable. No parent, indeed, should be allowed the liberty to bring up his child without education; but all the aid that Government can lend to adult education is to afford it opportunities. This is done in part by the plan of public libraries and museums, which, however, have scarcely begun to be established nationally.

The question of principle is already given up: instruction in drawing by the Schools of Design and the Department of Practical Art, are acknowledgments of the principle. To facilitate the operations of this department, drawing copies and models will be furnished at half-price to public schools and institutions. A body of teachers is being organised "who shall visit *schools* possessing these objects, and demonstrate to the *masters* and *mistresses* how to use them."[53] Shall they be sent to *Mechanics' Institutes?* If not, why not? The only answer that can be made is, that the majority of Mechanics' Institutes possess no teachers to receive the instruction. Where instruction in drawing is given,

[53] Address of Henry Cole, Esq., November 24th, 1852.

we think Institutions should, like public schools, receive the advantages of the superior system.

Mr. Cole anticipates, as a consequence of teaching a knowledge of form and colour to boys and girls, that in time a demand will be created for schools of a more advanced character. "When a neighbourhood," says he, "is sensible of this want, and makes its desire known to this department, we shall endeavour to be ready to aid. . . . . We will provide a collection of casts and models at half the cost, we will recommend a qualified teacher, and guarantee a certain income to him for a limited period, until the school becomes self-supporting." The constituency *needing* a teacher, already exists in the Mechanics' Institutes. If an Institute should ask for the services of such a teacher, guaranteeing a fair quota of his salary, would they be granted? If not, again we ask, why not? Is it, in the new scheme of industrial instruction which now "looms in the future," intended to throw overboard the Mechanics' Institutes? Mr. Cole speaks of these schools of art as probably becoming connected with local museums and libraries. *No mention is made of Mechanics' Institutes.* Yet what is requisite to make these Institutes that which they were proposed to be at their first foundation, and which is their greatest deficiency now, *schools of industrial instruction?* Precisely the aid which is now being offered by the Department of Practical Art, only instead of being limited to design, to embrace also the different branches of science required in the arts.

The *Athenæum*, in making one of the earliest announcements which have appeared on the subject of the proposed Industrial University, thus concisely states some of its leading features:—"When once the scheme is got into operation in London, a vast net-work of affiliated schools of industry will have to be established all over the country. These provincial schools, founded on a common model, but varying in their details according to the nature of the occupations followed in each locality, will stand in a somewhat similar relation to the central institution that Eton and Rugby do to Oxford or to Cambridge. The rudiments of a sound industrial education will be given to all the pupils in the former; while those who are intended for higher courses of instruction — men who propose to become masters, overseers, and managers of industrial establishments — will be prepared for the higher range of duties at the Metropolitan University. By these means, the whole industrial education of our population may be superintended, accelerated, and ultimately secured to such an extent, as shall put them at least on the same level of opportunity with the intelligently trained workmen who issue from the Gewerbe Institut of Berlin or the Conservatoire at Paris. The results, when this level shall have been gained, must be committed to the comparative natural genius and aptitudes of the several rivals."[54]

Now what we would propose is, to render every Mechanics' Institution a branch College of the proposed Industrial University. Let the "affiliated schools of industry" be formed on the basis of the Mechanics' Institute, or rather let the two be incorporated. The pupils of the Institute would form the nucleus for the extended scheme of instruction. Let not the same blunder be made here as with the Schools of Design, and two rival establishments be set up, each weakening the other, instead of one efficient institute to carry the common objects into adequate operation.

Inefficient as the Institutes may be as means of industrial instruction, they afford the best instrumentality for introducing an improved system. Moreover, the opposition to Government assistance would be increased

54 Athenæum, August 14th, 1852.

ten-fold if it were to *supersede* the Mechanics' Institutes instead of *helping* them.

The extent to which Government ought to aid adult instruction, and the means of doing so, are questions of expediency and detail, but very important. As the funds it dispenses are raised from the whole community, they should only be expended upon those objects in which, directly or indirectly, the whole community is interested, producing the largest possible result with a minimum expenditure. They should be applied so as to aid and stimulate local exertions, not to supersede and paralyse them. Too often Government aid has not followed these common-sense principles. Large salaries and little work, wages paid by day-work and not by piece-work, the local committee powerless, the Board in London omnipotent, endless schedules, forms, returns, rules, regulations, and terrible inspectors, — such, to our unofficial intellect, seems to be the usual plan for getting the thing *not* done. Town councils would be suitable bodies to afford funds when public education is more advanced; but we have no hopes from them at present. They have already the power to establish museums and libraries, — a power of which they do not avail themselves. The truth is, they represent the *ignorant prejudices*, quite as much as the good sense, of their constituents; and a good many of the represented think the highest merit in the representative is to vote against a tax. The party placard is never "Vote for Smith and Good Government," but "Vote for Smith and Economy;" which means, that said Smith is under no pretence to put his hand into the voter's pocket.

The best available mode of assisting Mechanics' Institutes, therefore, seems to be by means of a parliamentary grant. The more essential objects contemplated by these institutions are so indissolubly connected with the greatness of England and the well-being of her population, that it is of the highest importance to secure permanence in their action. At present they are at the mercy of every accident. If bad times come, — and in a country dependent on commerce and manufacturers they must often come, the operative's means of training ought not to cease because his employment is diminished. Rather ought he to have a refuge wherein he might profitably improve his involuntary leisure. He may forego what we have ventured to call the "luxuries" of the Institute, but he should have no inducement and no pretext for neglecting its essentials. Like our universities, colleges, and free grammar schools, to which, despite all their abuses[45], England owes no small portion of her greatness, they should help to keep alive, in the breasts of our population, the taste for art, science, and literature, when luxury, political strife, or national danger almost extinguishes the love for such pursuits.

Still more is it essential to adopt some means which will increase the efficiency of these Institutes. It may be said with truth, that Mechanics' Institutes have largely multiplied of late years, but scarcely if at all improved. Now what they need, is precisely that which Government can best and most legitimately give, the means of improving their educational efficiency. Any attempt to set up rival institutions would fail, and we think deservedly, unless the attempt to improve the present ones had been previously tried without success. What is wanted is to increase the efficiency of existing organisations, not to create new ones. It would be hard

55 The defects of such corporations, their resistance to improvement, and abuse of patronage, are sometimes cited as arguments against such endowments. Arguments from analogy are very fallacious, unless the conditions involved are the same. In former times, the element of public opinion had little force, responsibility to popular control no existence. These agencies will prevent repetitions of the mistakes of our ancestors; nay, they are even now remedying their consequences. Public opinion will bring them into accordance with the knowledge and wants of the times, and our age must supplement them by those larger and more comprehensive institutions required, now that knowledge is no longer the luxury of a few, but the right of all.

to find a new body in each large town, either so devoted to the object, or so able to carry it out with intelligence, as the Committee of the Mechanics' Institutes. Give these Institutions funds, give them trained teachers, but do not let us have the management in London and the master setting the local committee at defiance, because the conditions of his appointment are determined independently of them.

Had one half of the funds spent in the Schools of Design been granted to Mechanics' Institutions, on condition of carrying out the same objects, the success these Institutions have already achieved in their own architectural and mechanical drawing-classes is a sufficient warrant that ten times that which the Schools of Design have done would have been done by them. The course we recommend, was in fact pointed out when the Schools of Design were originated. The Committee of the Yorkshire Union of Mechanics' Institutes, in their Report for 1843 observe: —

"The Mechanics' Institutions of Leeds and Liverpool, having applied for grants of casts, books, &c., and for pecuniary aid to the drawing-schools already existing in those institutions, have been refused on the ground that the Schools of Design ought to be altogether separate and independent institutions. Your Committee cannot see any sufficient advantage in this independence to counterbalance its disadvantages. The multiplying of institutions is often a great evil, as dividing both the funds and the talents which can be appropriated to their support, diminishing the attractions which they are able to offer to the public, and establishing two or more feeble institutions instead of one that is vigorous and flourishing. Where a Mechanics' Institution already exists, with a good drawing-class, the effect of establishing a separate School of Design, would probably be to take away nearly all the pupils of the drawing-class, and perhaps some other members of the Mechanics' Institution, who without obtaining better instruction in the art of design than might have been obtained if the Institution had received a grant from the parliamentary fund, lose all the other advantages of an intellectual and moral kind, to be derived from the library and lectures.

"It is not likely that many pupils would belong to the School of Design and the Mechanics' Institute at the same time, as the subscription to the former is high, namely 4*s*. a month for the morning pupils, and 2*s*. per month for the evening pupils. It may also be feared that the local patronage given to the Schools of Design, will, in many cases be withdrawn from the Mechanics' Institutes.

"Whilst, therefore, your Committee would give all praise to the object which the School of Design has in view, namely, the promotion of taste in the designing of patterns for our various manufactures, and the cultivation of the fine arts generally, they cannot but think that that object would have been more effectually attained, and without injury to a most valuable class of institutions, but rather to their benefit, if grants had been made under proper conditions and securities to the Mechanics' and Literary Institutions already in being."

These anticipations respecting the Schools of Design have been justified by the event, and Government seems now disposed to fall into the other extreme. No more Schools of Design are to be established, and those already in existence are to be thrown upon their own resources as soon as possible. There can be no objection, provided efficient aid is furnished in other ways; but it cannot be called an improvement, if, instead of *unwise* support to art-education, *no* support is substituted. The steps already taken by the Department of Practical Art are worthy of all commendation, and the principle on which it proposes to promote art-education is one that might be safely adopted in extending industrial instruction generally. It is "to afford partial aid, to encourage, but not to supersede public exertions in art." In the distribution of examples they furnish them to public schools and institutions at half the prime cost, considering that, "as the indiscriminate gift of examples to all applicants might lead to abuse, it is necessary to require some guarantee that the examples will be duly appreciated, which the mere request to have them does not imply."

We think that Mechanics' Institutes should be furnished with the outfit of apparatus, library of reference, models, drawings, &c., essential to industrial instruction upon similar conditions. But more than this is required to render the Institutes efficient, namely, the payment of qualified teachers. An annual grant might be given to all institutions willing to give a certain prescribed class of instruction. After the first expenses of the establishment have been furnished, the amount granted might be contingent on the number of pupils actually receiving instruction and able to pass a satisfactory examination. Make it dependent upon the *result*, and then no interference would be required with the management, for, provided the effect desired takes place, the *how* is of secondary consequence. As the efficiency of education increased, the amount granted might be diminished, until its support could with safety be thrown upon the local municipal authority, or even be made self-supporting.

It is quite possible that some Institutes might so little recognise their primary educational duties as to decline or neglect to use such advantages when offered, and in that case they should be extended to any other public body willing to fulfil the conditions. We only insist that the Mechanics' Institutes should have the first chance. From the great deficiency among our labouring classes of even such elementary knowledge as reading, writing, and arithmetic, these subjects should be included in the class of instruction specially paid for by the grant. It would only be a slight amends for our past neglect, and some endeavour to recover lost time. Teachers for the simpler departments of learning would readily be found, if once directors had the means of paying them. In the more advanced classes the same methods which the Government is adopting for the preparation of day-school teachers, and teachers for the Department of Practical Art, would provide them in other branches of knowledge. But the sole appointment and control should rest in those who conduct the Institution.

Such a plan would enable us to have the advantages of centralisation and localisation without their defects. Those who know the bigotry, sloth, and stupid prejudices, which education of any sort has to encounter everywhere, save in the centre of our large towns, will not undervalue the assistance which men, elevated by rank and education, and labouring for the general interests of instruction, can confer; while by leaving the management of the Institute in the hands of a local body, and rendering it partly dependent on local support, the evils of bureaucracy are avoided, and the people taught more and more to rely upon themselves. We should deprecate the exclusive domination of either principle, but assuredly the danger in the present day is not from centralisation, but, in truth, from trusting to local effort that which it will not, because in the present state of knowledge it cannot, perform.

It is all very well to talk of the Institutes being "self-supporting." It rounds a speech to talk of the virtue of "self-reliance." But practical men who wish for *results*, who want those results to be independent of temporary excitement and occasional spasmodic revivals, will prefer permanent improvement to rhetoric. The

London Mechanics' Institute was started upon such self-reliant principles, that even the applause at the offer of a professional gentleman to give a course of lectures *gratis*, was objected to! Government help to education was denounced. "Men," said the *Mechanics' Magazine*, "had better be without education than be educated by their rulers." The rich were told, that they "knew nothing of what the lower classes need, nor what is fitting for them. They know, indeed, too well what is proper for them as *subjects*, as *tax-paying machines*, as slaves, but not what is suitable for them as labourers and as men." The Glasgow Institute, on its secession from Anderson's University, started with great professions of self-reliance; it had, besides, the advantage of possessing a large accumulation of property; but it was compelled to rely very largely on the support of the wealthy. All words are vain when they do not represent *facts*, so all this vapouring about self-reliance came to nothing. It was not till the Institutions almost gave up direct scientific instruction, that they were able to pay their way, and hardly then. Nobody denies that it would be better if Institutions giving really good scientific instruction to the working classes could be self-supporting, any more than one doubts that it would be better if every parent could pay a good schoolmaster to teach his children. Neither does any one deny that Government has made, and is likely to make, mistakes. What then? Will any one contend that a homily on self-reliance, or a tirade on governmental blunders, as premises of the argument, will prove that scientific education can be provided without government assistance; or, what comes to the same thing, that Government cannot advantageously *assist* (for no one proposes it should entirely provide) such instruction? Government is a machine, liable to defects, and sometimes to a break-down Let us diminish its defects, improve its powers, but, in the name of all experience and common sense, let us not cast an imperfect tool away, where we have none to substitute in its place.

A vast obstacle to the success of many Mechanics' Institutes, especially in the smaller towns, is the want of a building; and this often in places where excellent buildings, erected by means of the assistance from Government, already exist. A clause in the deeds rendering these buildings available for evening instruction would be a useful condition of future grants, as a very slight adaptation of these buildings would fit them for the purposes of the Mechanics' Institutes. It is a pity that, because of the whim of one or two persons whose position, rather than any interest they ever showed in education, gives them power, as trustees of the building, to cause them to be shut up and dark, while the Mechanics' Institute is stuck in a garret or a loft.

In several towns, the town-hall has been appropriated to the purpose of the Institute, for lectures. If aid were offered as we propose, it would be found very easy to add class-rooms, library, &c., to complete the functions of the Institute.

It may be useful to point out to the directors of these Institutes, that, by making a day-school a part of the Institution, they have already the power to obtain the Government grant to the erection of a building, a matter of no slight importance when the present imperfect accommodation of most of them is considered. The Patricroft Institute, near Manchester, built at an expense of 1000*l*., received 300*l*. grant towards it. Mr. Thomas Hogg, formerly Secretary of the Lancashire and Cheshire Union of Mechanics' Institutes, thus refers to it:—

"It will be seen that at one Institution the sum of 300*l*. was obtained, in aid of the building-fund, from the Committee of Council on Education. This sum was of course granted because a day-school was to be opened; and in the size and arrangement of the rooms &c., the plans for Government schools had to be complied with. In the trust-deed, no degrading or tyrannical conditions are imposed by the acceptance of Government assistance; but these conditions are simply intended to ensure that the building shall be used for the purposes for which it was erected. The building cannot be mortgaged, but the trustees have to give a bond on it to the amount of the grant, the said bond being of no effect so long as the terms of the trust-deed are complied with; two conditions which the public will see are quite reasonable and necessary in dispensing the public money. I would earnestly press this subject on the attention of the various boards of directors, as I believe that the receipt of Government assistance, in the same manner as at Patricroft, involves no sacrifice whatever of the independence or free action of the Institution, while it most effectually aids its operations and extends education among the people. Nor can I see that any other schools have greater claims than day-schools in connection with Mechanics' Institutions, for assistance towards the erection of buildings, from a grant which is made up of contributions from all classes of the community."[56] With our present educational deficiencies, every possible opportunity of establishing a day-school should be made use of.[57] There is no risk in establishing them, as they may be easily made self-supporting.

Then the pupils, being admitted to the privileges of the Institution, learn to appreciate its advantages, and are likely to prove its firmest supporters. The day-school being connected with the Mechanics' Institute enables the working man to share indirectly in the management of his children's education. It permits the studies of the day-school and of the evening-classes to

[56] Circular of 15th May, 1850, entitled "Improvement of Mechanics' Institutions."

[57] History of Adult Education, pp. 93. 102. 134.

be adapted to each other ; one the preparation, the other the perfecting, of the same process.

In large and even moderate-sized towns the distance of the Institute from the homes of the working classes is a considerable hindrance to their regular attendance, except on occasions of extraordinary interest. In such cases it would be desirable to open branches in connection with the principal Institute of the town. It would generally be easy to secure some large school-room for the purpose, wherein the members might receive their class-instruction, with the privilege of attending the lectures and library of the parent Institute. The business would be managed, and the teachers be paid and appointed, by the central committee. When the population of the district had so far felt the benefits of the classes as to be able to support and manage them for themselves, they should do so, and the other features of the Institute, as library and lectures, might be added, so as to form an independent Institute. At present, however, the problem is to bring the skill and experience acquired by the committee of our larger institutions to bear upon the outlying masses of population engaged in manufactures, and, since they will not go to the school, to bring the school to them. They reside in the suburbs of the town, and have rarely a sufficient number of persons among them of adequate zeal and ability to manage an Institute with success. The establishment of evening-classes, lectures, &c., in connection with the various places of worship, is a great step in the right direction. As is well known, however, the mass of the operative classes does not belong to any religious denomination, numbers having a thorough distaste for each and all of them, the majority being quite indifferent. Branch Institutes form, therefore, the only machinery capable of reaching them. So long as the large Institutes can hardly pay their way, they can scarcely be expected to initiate movements which, for some time at least, might, and probably would, prove unremunerative. But grant them adequate assistance for carrying out their educational objects, and their committees would be very glad to extend their operations in the way indicated.

There is one advantage which would arise from adequate assistance to Mechanics' Institutes, on the part of the state, over and above that of diffusing scientific instruction among the people, which of course is the primary one. But another one is too important to be overlooked. By improving the position of the scientific teacher, we should help to extend the domain of science itself. It is well known that, with one or two brilliant exceptions, we are falling behind other civilised nations in the path of original research and scientific discovery.[58] From various causes our wealthy and aristocratic classes, once honourably distinguished by the numerous instances they furnished of men devoted to scientific investigation, have ceased to be so. Various causes have been assigned, such as the system of education pursued in our colleges and universities; the neglect of patronage, on the part of the Government, which has not only done next to nothing for science, but constantly filled up the situations requiring extensive knowledge in certain departments by persons notoriously in want of it; the abuses of our learned societies, which have admitted their members rather because they could pay the fees than because they could add anything to the stores of science, — these and other causes have been assigned for our neglect of science, and probably all have been operative. However, the fact is certain, that in this country science, like virtue, must be its own reward, for no vocation is worse treated, or has a less chance of yielding bread to its followers. Unless favoured with independent sources of support, no

[58] Preliminary Discourse on the Study of Natural History, part 4., by Wm. Swainson, Cabinet Cyclopedia.

man, whatever be his genius or willingness to make sacrifices, can afford to run the risk of such pursuits. It is not likely that men will devote themselves to science when the reward of years of laborious study will most probably be poverty and neglect. An adequate provision for lecturers and teachers to the masses of our industrial population, if it would not remedy the evil, would do much to mitigate it. The means of living would be found for the poor student of science, and the path of honourable distinction opened to him. At least, we should not see men versed in half a dozen sciences glad to secure engagements at one-fourth the sum they would have obtained, if, in lieu of these acquirements, they had been able to warble a few ballads. Mr. John Stuart Mill has pointed out the desirableness of the state affording some provision for those experiments and investigations, which, however valuable to the public, are not likely to afford those engaged in them the means of subsistence. "There should be," says he, "a mode of insuring to the public the services of scientific discoverers, and perhaps of some other classes of *savans*, by affording them the means of support consistently with devoting a sufficient portion of time to their peculiar pursuits. The most effectual plan, and at the same time the least liable to abuse, seems to be that of conferring professorships with duties of instruction attached to them. The occupation of teaching a branch of knowledge, at least in its higher departments, is a help rather than an impediment to the systematic cultivation of the subject itself. In the case of a lecturer in a great institution the public at large has the means of judging, if not of the quality of the teaching, at least of the talents of the teacher; and it is more difficult to misemploy the power of appointment to such an office than to job in pensions and salaries to persons not so directly before the public eye." [59]

[59] Political Economy, vol. ii. p. 546.

Before quitting the subject of finances of Mechanics' Institutions, we would call attention to a point of the highest importance, and to which little attention has been given by their managers: we allude to the regular collection of the unpaid subscriptions. The transactions of the Institute are not like the sale effected by a shopkeeper, who receives his payment when handing over the commodity he is selling. Nor is the association like any of those in which the member, having paid a part of the original capital, or having subscribed to the funds, loses the sum he subscribed, or the benefits of all his previous contribution, by ceasing to be a member. There is no pecuniary temptation rendering it incumbent upon him to make a similar sacrifice to that which he would make to raise the payment to his lodge or friendly society. He may leave now, and join next month or next year, and he will be readmitted on the same footing as he left it. The subscription to the Mechanics' Institute is like the rates levied for gas, water, highways, &c. There are few people who do not estimate these things as cheaply purchased at the price they pay for them, — yet fancy the numberless defaulters and the mass of arrears there would be, if the payments for these services were not regularly called for by persons specially appointed! It is still worse with Mechanics' Institutes, because the want of the aid which they render is less felt, though in reality greater. The date when subscriptions are due is easily forgotten, arrears accumulate, until to pay them up becomes a formidable affair to a poor man, and he leaves the Institution. The Institute not only loses its members by allowing them to fall into arrear; it loses funds, and its power to offer attractions is diminished in like proportion. A large number, say 10 to 20 per cent., regularly fail to renew their subscriptions, their places being supplied by fresh members. In some places not one half pay their subscriptions till called for. The secret of the extinction of many an Institute started under flourishing auspices is attributable to this cause alone. From inquiries made on the subject from different Institutes, we have found, that while very few committees attend to it, because unaware of its importance, those which do derive the greatest advantage from the practice of collecting all the subscriptions immediately when due. At the Institution which contains the greatest number of members in the kingdom, — we mean Leeds, — it is an invariable rule.

Seeing of what essential importance it is to the welfare of an Institute to render the general body of members as little fluctuating as possible, something of a proprietary interest should exist therein. The best plan of effecting it appears to be the creation of a body of proprietary members, the larger the better, who, in consideration of paying a pound or two pounds entrance in addition to their regular subscription, shall be entitled to some small additional privilege, as the free admission of a member of their family to the lectures. The proprietary right should be transferable if the member left the town, but forfeited in the event of the member failing to pay his subscription. The plan has been advantageous to the Leeds Institute by discouraging fluctuations in the most influential portion of the members. In the management of the Institution, however, proprietary members should have no special control; for nothing in the rules of these societies is more objectionable or hurtful than any invidious distinctions.

There is a class of duties and services in the conduct of these institutions, that ought to be paid for, but which seldom is. The duty of collecting subscriptions is one, the cleaning and attending to the Institute is another, the keeping the accounts, delivery of the library books, and other mechanical duties, are of this class. If we cannot rely upon gratuitous service alone for teachers, still less can we expect it here. The teacher has the consciousness of filling a superior position; he feels that he is communicating a direct benefit to the taught; he has the gratification of a generous task performed, and a corresponding gratitude awakened. But how shall the mechanical drudgery of the Institute have any exalted sentiments attached to it? and, unless it has, it cannot be well performed without fee or reward. The wonder is, how so large an amount of work gets done, as is performed by men who, after a day's toil, go and labour yet two hours more, to help what they feel to be a good cause. But it is the falsest economy to entrust such duties to honorary officers. Pay for the service, and you can choose its character and its amount. Pay for it, and you can require it to be properly performed. But when it is not paid for, you cannot complain of deficiencies, for whatever was done was more than you had a right to expect.

This principle applies to the smallest Institution as well as to the largest, but to the latter it will bear a still more extensive application. Committees are apt to be fond of over-legislation, and consume an enormous amount of time to very little purpose, or at least to a purpose that could be quite as well fulfilled without.

It would, perhaps, be expedient to have a managing director in addition to the secretary, as the railway companies have. Most committees waste so much time in talk that they have no time to do business, though it passes under the name. The amount of business done, as a general rule, is in the inverse ratio of the number present at a committee. Large Institutes can afford to pay for superior managing talent, and the greatest economy for the Institutes and themselves will be secured by doing so. By the course we recommend, a greater degree of permanency would be realised by the Institute. It often happens that an Institute is started by a benevolent self-denying person, who is the very soul of it. So long as he labours for it, it goes on well; but other engagements, or some of the many changes of life, remove him, and it dies. Every body had got so accustomed to lean on him, that when he is gone they never think of doing anything for themselves. With paid officers this is not likely to occur, since an efficient help is much more easily replaced. Having secured good managing talent, they should trust it. In all associations, it is desirable to obtain those advantages which are possessed by establishments conducted merely with a view to private advantage. Divided power means divided responsibility, and opens the door to all sorts of jobbing and abuses. Where the paid officers do all the work, and the committee take all the credit, the former feel no stimulus to introduce improvements; and if any are proposed calculated to throw additional labour on them, they will often throw effectual obstacles in the way. The greatest care should be exercised in the selection of such officers, and a constant account of their acts required from them; but while the responsibilities of action are imposed, the due award of success should not be withheld. If these institutions would secure the success of commercial undertakings, they must copy their principle of management. A dozen gentlemen need not meet to debate upon every trifle. A great step in the right direction is the division of the committee into sub-committees, each taking charge of a department of the Institute. Under this plan, the library and news-room fall to one section, the classes and day-school to another, the lectures to a fourth, and so on; and the result is an amount of work utterly unattainable under the system which brings everything under the deliberation of the whole committee.

A vital condition of the successful influence of an Institute is publicity. To ascertain whether an Institute was well known, we have tried the experiment in towns we have visited of inquiring *where* it was? No one but those who do so, can conceive how strange the very name of the Institute is to the vast mass of the population. That which is interesting to ourselves, we are apt to fancy must be so to every body else. Puffery is always discreditable, and often self-defeating; but an Institute should at least take as much trouble to make its advantages known as a tradesman does his wares. They should not lose a single member through ignorance of what they offer. Employers would frequently offer facilities for such announcements, and at suitable opportunities point them out to those who serve them, if its importance were explained to them.

The management of Institutes should be as popular as possible. The committee should be composed, whereever possible, both of employers and of the working classes. The former have more administrative talent and experience, and are more accustomed to conduct large organisations and introduce improvements; the latter are needed to secure due attention to the interest of the operative members, and to give them confidence in the management. The question would be one of some importance as to what restrictions should be put on the power of the members, if experience had not shown that in the large majority of Institutes not a tenth of the members take the slightest interest in the matter, or even attend the annual meeting for electing the directors. This arises in the main from the conviction of the members, that the managers do the best they can with the means at their disposal. Though in ordinary cases the franchise of the members is unused, it is a useful safety-valve on extraordinary occasions. It disarms the management of the semblance of injustice, and stops the objections of cavillers among the working classes themselves. We have found it an effectual reply, when we have heard such Institutes accused of aristocratic exclusiveness, to point out that the Institute was based on "Universal suffrage, vote by ballot, and annual parliaments." And the fault therefore arose, not from those who did, but from those who did not, attend its meetings.

Another point of practical importance is the avoidance of debt. Debt is a state of disease, into which associated bodies are very liable to fall, and find it very difficult to recover from. The responsibility of incurring it is divided among the directors, and each therefore feels it less; but when debt does, as it always does, bring its inconvenience, each is ready to escape it, like the rats in the sinking ship. At least, no committee which has been acting imprudently, will readily find successors to take the consequences. The best mode of avoiding imprudent expenditure is to prepare at the beginning of the year an estimate of the probable income, and by this to regulate the amount to be expended upon each department of the Institute, rigidly adhering to the specific sum. By a strict observance of this rule, and a judicious management of the funds, many an Institute might clear off its weight of incumbrance, while the sum paid as interest would add largely to the power of the Institute.[60]

In concluding this part of the subject, we would observe, that though machinery is important, and organisation essential, to the prosperity of these Institutes, they are not everything. The spirit in which they are worked is even more important. If those who labour therein are actuated by high aims and an earnest purpose, they may perform wonders with even poor materials and opportunities. The dingy garret in which they offer the bread of knowledge to the ignorant, shall fill as worthy a purpose as the groves of Academus

60 By strict attention to this system of expenditure, the Leeds Institute has, out of its ordinary income, recently paid off 600*l.* of its mortgage debt, and 350*l.* of its floating debt, and is now quite clear of all debt whatever.

or the cloistered College. To their humble library, the anxious youth will come at the end of his daily labour, to feast on the "ample page, rich with the spoils of time;" and at their lectures—the lectures of self-taught men, unpolished in language perhaps, but rich in good common sense,—the young man who has grown up untaught, while sects have been scrambling for the privilege of teaching him, will hear words that will reach even his rude intellect, and awaken his better nature, and his wife and children will be the happier that he has heard those words. While we would desire that the externals of the Institute and its working machinery should be as good and efficient as possible, there should be a spirit of devotion in the workers, to ensure its success. If the final cause of such associations be but to provide cheap books, amusing lectures, and comfortable news-rooms, these things might be left to private enterprise. The appeal to the wealthy for their money, and to the illustrious for their advocacy, is a fraud. But if their promoters recognise the greatness of their vocation,—that, in the words of Sterling, "A man's whole business on earth, as to his own existence, is to cultivate himself; and his whole business, as to others, is to cultivate them,"—they will recognise the spirit in which they should labour. They will be content to work in any position in which they can be most useful, even though it should not be that which most redounds to their personal glory. They will rather be silent than make the Institute the arena for displaying their power of empty talk. And sooner than dissension should endanger its welfare, they will make almost any concession, trusting to Truth the ultimate vindication of her own power.

CHAPTER IV.

UNION OF INSTITUTES.

Having referred to the method by which each Institution may individually be best improved and developed, we proceed to consider in what way the collective action of a number of Institutes may be made conducive to the same end. Here, as in everything else, system and organisation give power; and the more complete and perfect this is, the greater the advantages to the respective Institutes. If, indeed, a combination of them were incapable of reflecting any benefit on the individual Institutes, there would still be ample reasons why such an organisation should exist. It is important that some minds should be occupied in the work of inspection, and in securing the general advancement of those objects at which Mechanics' and Literary Institutes aim. There should be men who, by their freedom from other occupation, position in life, superior culture, and strong sympathy with the cause of popular education, are fitted to watch over its general interests. They should at the same time be so familiar with the management of these institutions, as to give their labours a practical value.

The associations for diffusing knowledge among the people may, like the members of individual Institutes, derive stimulus and help from the sympathy of congenial pursuits. If we regard the individual societies as the arteries which carry the stream of intellectual life to the farthest verge of our land, the central body that connects them into one vast system may be likened to the heart, which receives the vitalised blood only to propel it round with freshened force and benefit. Nor, were the organisation perfect, should there be the smallest village, or most insignificant hamlet, in our island, with its little library or humble mutual improvement society, that would fail to enjoy the benefits of such a central body, just as in a healthy body the smallest capillaries share the heart's force as well as the largest arteries.

The perception of the advantages to be derived from the combination of the Institutes for adult education, has led to various attempts at realisation. We say attempts, for as yet no Union of Institutes in this country has attained the ends it proposed to itself, still less those which it ought to fulfil. The cause of this it is not difficult to discover. The body partook of more than the weakness of the members. With, in general, no other source to rely on for funds than the contributions of crippled societies, it is not to be wondered at that the Unions were paralysed for want of funds. In the management of any Union of Institutes, however limited its objects, there must be a considerable amount of correspondence, and of mechanical drudgery and detail — a class of service not likely to be well, or continuously performed, by an unpaid amateur; but in no single Union yet established, have the *Institutes* contributed as much to the central body as would enable them to engage an ordinary clerk.

The union of educational societies for mutual advantage had been extensively adopted in America (before it was even thought of in England), under the name of the Lyceum system. With the rapidity of development which seems to attend every thing American, the plan, from its first proposal in 1826 in the American Journal of Education, had in 1831 grown into an actual union of not less than eight hundred or one thousand town Lyceums, fifty or sixty county Lyceums, and a general union of the whole under the denomination of the "National Lyceum." The county Lyceums met half-yearly, to consider the reports from the town Lyceums. The county Lyceum obtained from the funds furnished by the town Lyceums a county library, apparatus, and models. Collections in natural history and mineralogy were furnished principally by the labour of the members of the town Lyceums. The state Lyceums were composed of delegates from the county Lyceums, and held meetings annually. The object of the state Lyceums was to "hear reports from the county Lyceums on the progress of education in every part of the state, to collect and combine facts of a useful character, to publish results and statements of former experiments, to suggest new ones, to confer and propose prizes and rewards,—in a word, to act in every particular as a sort of provincial board, in aid of the national one (as the National Lyceum may be called), for the promotion of general education."

The National Lyceum is to the state Lyceums what these are to the county Lyceums, and these again to the town Lyceums; the organisation of the strength and experience of the whole, for the benefit of the individual bodies. At the meeting of the National Lyceum, delegates from the state Lyceums are assembled; and, where no state Lyceum exists from the county, or even the town Lyceums, and also from the several classes of public teachers, papers are read on important subjects connected with education.

Mr. Wyse (late M.P. for Waterford), from whose paper on the Lyceum system of America[61] the foregoing facts have been taken, brought the subject of these Unions prominently before the attention of the public, and recommended the application of the same principle to this country in a modified form. The first practical

[61] Second Publication of the Central Society of Education, 1838. So long a period having elapsed since this account was published, information as to its present state is very much to be desired.

attempt to establish a union of Mechanics' Institutes was made by Mr. Edward Baines, who, in an article in the "Leeds Mercury" of the 26th September, 1837, proposed the formation of the West Riding Union of Mechanics' Institutes. The plan was favourably received; and, at a meeting of delegates authorised by thirteen societies, the Union was duly formed on the 11th December, 1837. Mr. Edward Baines, who was chosen to be the first president, has continued to fill that office to the present time. By his personal labours, and the prominence he has given through the press to the subject of Mechanics' Institutes, he has contributed very largely to their diffusion.

One of the most prominent of Mr. Baines's original proposals was, that the Union should engage one or more permanent lecturers to visit the Institutes, to give a regular course of instruction on such subjects as Chemistry, Mechanics, Political Economy, &c. The lecturers were to be sufficient to supply the Institutions with a complete course of instruction on each subject, and thus, at least, carry out the object which the earliest promoters of Mechanics' Institutes had contemplated. Unfortunately this idea could not be accomplished, and yet remains to be realised. As the next best thing, the Union made arrangements with lecturers for concurrent courses of lectures to such Institutes as were able to afford their services.

It was thought that, by securing to a lecturer a series of consecutive engagements in contiguous Institutes, some reduction on lecture fees, and a large reduction in travelling expenses, might have been effected. The plan succeeded in the case of a few well-known and very popular lecturers; but afterwards, when the system had to depend upon the ordinary demand for paid lectures, it broke down completely. As we have said, the engagement of a paid lecturer is the exception, and not the rule, with the large majority of Institutes. The Yorkshire Union now confines itself to offering, in the Annual Report, a list of lecturers with whom the united Institutions may correspond when wanting their services. In April, 1841, the Union was changed from the West Riding into the Yorkshire Union of Mechanics' Institutes. The following comparison of its state at the formation, with its present condition, is interesting:—

	Institutions.	Members.	Books.
1837	13	2661	8,373 in 9 of the Institutes.
1852	123	20,000	100,000 ,,

In 1849, a new plan was tried. The sum of nearly 200*l.* per annum was raised by subscriptions among the gentry of Yorkshire, for the purpose of employing a paid agent and lecturer. With but one lecturer for visiting 120 Institutions scattered over the whole of a large county, and that within the six winter months, each Institute cannot obtain more than one lecture per year. This is better than nothing, but too little to present a tolerably complete and connected view of any single topic. Being restricted to one set of Institutions, he has to lecture upon a greater variety of subjects than the most encyclopædic head could thoroughly master; the lectures are given at a large amount of time and labour to the lecturer, while the pecuniary cost to the Institute for travelling is heavy, owing to the visits not occurring in their topographical order.

The advantages of the Yorkshire Union are thus stated in the Report:—

" 1st. The publication of an annual report, embracing the principal features furnished by the experience of each Institution during the preceding year. The Report is the only permanent record of the history and progress of these Institutions. By its means each Institution is enabled to learn, from the experience of others, to secure the advantages, and avoid the mistakes, of similar

Institutions. It also extends the knowledge of them to persons by whom they were unknown, or not sufficiently valued, and leads to their formation in districts where no Institution exists. Along with the reports of the Institutions, the Central Committee send a general report containing such suggestions and remarks as they think useful.

"2nd. Affording Institutes facilities for obtaining lecturers. Local committees have but few opportunities of ascertaining the character and ability of professional lecturers. The Central Committee makes proper inquiry upon these points before recommending them.[62] The Report also records the names of gentlemen willing to give gratuitous lectures at the Institutes in their own neighbourhood. And, lastly, it offers the use of 100 original manuscript lectures, many of them characterised by great ability.

"3rd. The services of an agent or lecturer, who is paid principally by contributions from the nobility and gentry of Yorkshire. His duties are to deliver lectures; to assist in the formation of new Institutions, wherever openings present themselves; and to visit committees, when invited by them, for the sake of suggesting improvements in the constitution and management of the Institutions, or to assist at their annual meetings.

"4th. The annual meeting of delegates from each Institution, held every year in a different locality. At these meetings valuable information is often elicited, and mutual sympathy and encouragement given to further exertions.

"5th. The Central Committee are at all times ready to give their advice when it is desired, to revise the rules of new Institutions, and to aid, as far as in them lies, the general prosperity of each and all of them.

[62] Being connected with one of the largest Institutions, which is able to engage a great variety of lecturers, it has thus the still greater advantage of judging practically of the merits of each lecturer.

Considering that the subscriptions from the respective Institutes is (for the majority of them) only 10*s. per annum*[63], it is obvious that the advantages far transcend the pecuniary contributions.

We have cited the Yorkshire Union, because it is the first in order of time, and, with the exception of the Union of the Society of Arts, formed last year, the most important.

Several other Unions were formed, for the history of which we must refer to Dr. Hudson's work on adult education.[64] Most of them have become extinct, many of them almost as soon as formed.[65] Those that remain possess as yet so little cohesion and vitality, that the activity of one or two persons alone prevents them from sharing the same fate. Once a year, indeed, at their annual gatherings under the presidency of some distinguished friend of popular instruction, they waken up into renewed life; but, during the remainder of the year, their action is scarcely felt by the individual Institutes. These annual re-unions are indeed valuable; and, being held each year in a different town, realise advantages which a great gathering in London could not confer. A conference of the delegates of these Institutes, aided by distinguished men, imparts importance to the local Institute visited in the eyes of the inhabitants, and removes much of the ill-will and antagonism to which such societies are still liable. Then, again, the delegates, who are usually members of the committee of their own local Institute, go home, cheered on by that sym-

[63] Institutes having 70 members, or under, pay - 5*s.*
Institutes having above 70 members, and under 150, pay - - - 10*s.*
Institutes having above 150 members pay - 20*s.*

[64] P. 175—188.

[65] Those lately in existence were, the Lancashire and Cheshire Union, *extinct;* the Western Union, lately dissolved. The Midland Union now confines itself to holding annual meetings in the larger towns of the district, and promoting the formation of village Institutes. A Leicestershire Union was inaugurated on January 3rd, 1853, consisting of about fifteen Institutes. The Yorkshire Union and Northern Union still continue.

pathy which congregations of men for a common object always awaken. Sometimes they obtain practical hints of great importance, and learn to take larger views of the objects and operations of the Institutes; they see and feel themselves to be engaged in a great work, and they become more imbued with the spirit of exalted endeavour.[66]

The question meets us, Why have the Unions of Institutes not accomplished more? Is it because the objects at which they aimed are impracticable in themselves, or is it because they have not had the means to accomplish them? We venture to affirm the latter. Owing to the poverty of the Institutions, the conductors are apt to look upon every farthing contributed to the Unions as so much loss, unless an immediate equivalent is returned to them. Notwithstanding the very small subscription required from the Institutes, only nominally adequate to cover the trivial expenses of the Union, the subscriptions are always in arrear. The balance-sheet for 1852 of the Yorkshire Union shows that 30*l.* was the total sum received in one year from 120 Institutes (an average of 5*s.* each), and the balance due to the treasurer at the beginning of the year, 69*l.* 6*s.*, was increased to 82*l.* 10*s.* 2*d.* at the end of it. Even to the fund for the payment of a lecturer to this Union, out of the nine or ten which subscribed to it on its establishment in 1849, seven have ceased to subscribe, the reason assigned in every case being the lowness of their own funds.[67] The

[66] So powerful an engine of improvement was the American Lyceum system in this respect, and so beneficial these conferences of teachers and others interested in education, that, according to their Report quoted by Mr. Wyse, "the character of a vast number of schools has been entirely changed, and that, too, without any additional expense of time or money. Numerous towns are now realising double, from their appropriations to schools, of what they received two years since. The same teachers and the same pupils do twice the work very recently performed by them, in consequence of the management and aid received by them from Lyceums."

[67] In the Northern Union, the total subscription received from the branches, in 1852, was 16*l.* 10*s.* The balance due to the treasurer was increased from 12*l.* 11*s.* 9*d.* to 21*l.* 15*s.* 9*d.*

Union of Institutes formed in connection with the Society of Arts, has commenced by charging the Institutes joining it two guineas per annum. This sum, small as it is when compared with the advantages which such a union cannot but confer, will place it utterly out of the power of the smaller Institutes to join it. We fear, also, that when the novelty has passed away, no small number of the "220 Institutes, containing 90,000 members," will cease to belong to it, unless it offer advantages greater than it has yet proposed, or than it will be capable of doing without aid is afforded it of a more practical character than that tendered it on the 18th of May, 1852, valuable as that doubtless was.

The advantages which a union of Institutes should confer, are of a twofold nature:—

1st. Those which belong to the general interests of all such Institutes;

2nd. Those which have special reference to each individual Institution.

The benefits which a central body, acting for the general interests of adult education, might confer, are in our opinion quite as numerous and important as those it can offer to the individual Institutes. Unfortunately, they are not likely to be equally valued by the recipients, except in those moments of emergency when the general want becomes their own special case. Most local committees would promptly refuse their contributions to a central body which solicited funds to enable it to obtain legislative exemption for local taxation, unless its own Institution were at that moment subjected to a heavy demand for local rates. Is it, therefore, likely that services of this important character will be rendered in a constant and effectual manner, unless the central body can derive funds from other than a local source? One of the primary duties of a central body, such as we assume should exist, is to become aggressive; by which we mean, that it should direct attention to those places where no means of adult education exist, with a view of organising such. If it be the duty of a central body to improve less advanced societies by the example of those which are more so, then, *à fortiori*, it behoves it to help places where no such means exist at all. There are numerous places (far more than many may imagine) where neither institute, nor night school, nor library exists, and where the sole resort of the working man, if he will not stay at his (often uninviting) home, must be either the street-corner or the public-house. Such destitute places may be classified into small towns capable of supporting a Mechanics' Institute, with its machinery of classes, lectures, &c., and into villages unequal to this, but which might furnish a good number of subscribers to a library. In many small towns no institution exists, simply because nobody has taken the trouble to start it. If you talk to one of the inhabitants on the subject, he will tell you that it "has been mentioned, and Sir Somebody offered to give 5*l.* and some books, but nobody else took it up; so it fell through." You suggest that they are quite as capable of supporting an Institute as some other place which you name. "Yes," he replies, "but then they have no public spirit here, though perhaps something might be done." And everybody's business being nobody's, there the matter would end. Now, it is precisely here that the Union ought to step in. Let it send its agent or representative, a man of good address, whose ability would reflect as much credit on the Union as the Union on him, and a man earnest in his work, for without this, all other qualifications are in vain. He would summon the inhabitants together, and obtain the presence or sanction of the principal residents where possible, explain the importance of adult education, the nature and objects of Mechanics' Institutions, and the desirableness of each inhabitant helping so good a work. He would get a committee formed to canvass for subscribers and donations of money and books, and assist them in explaining the object to the principal inhabitants. He would furnish them with a model of rules whereby to frame their own, a good catalogue of books and their prices, carefully considered plans for keeping their accounts, and whatever other information might be needed. Knowing the difficulties of such undertakings, he would occasionally visit them, till the society had got thoroughly established. This is no imaginary plan. It has been done, and frequently. Towns that slumbered long without one sign of intellectual activity, have had an institution established on a prosperous basis. The means of diffusing a healthy mental and moral atmosphere around have been brought into existence by the active exertions, for three or four days, of one man, and he a stranger.

But there are other places with a tolerable population, where no such means of adult instruction could exist, for there are no persons willing or able to conduct one. The squire, or the clergyman, is the only person who could render effectual help, but in not one instance out of a score do they look with favour upon the plan—well, indeed, if they do not oppose it as "new-fangled and dangerous." They have never seen the labourer in any other state than that of besotted ignorance, and they care not to believe any other possible. Intelligence, as they conceive of it, means insubordination, while literary taste of the humblest kind is but another name for laziness and discontent. The only growth the peasant acquires is that of the body, his pleasures are rude sports, and the tap-room of the village public-house his highest elysium. Those who have only lived in towns, and become familiarised with the mental activity there prevailing, cannot realise the dull stupidity of village life. Gas-light, house-drainage, and similar advantages of civilisation, are eschewed, even when offered; and efforts to help the rural population are often treated as selfish attempts to take advantage of them. This state of things of course has many exceptions. There is no reason, however, why it should exist at all. Let but the Government of the country do its duty in respect of the education of the young, and many of the worst evils of our village life will pass away. At least its sluggishness, its sensualism, its tenacious adherence to antiquated absurdities, will be diminished. Much, however, might be done by really efficient unions. They might send an occasional lecturer, who should teach, in a clear and interesting manner, the first principles of science, explain the importance of cleanliness of person and dwelling, of ventilation, of sobriety, and the relation of these things to moral happiness, as well as physical comfort.

The Union might also give important aid to the cause of adult education by the establishment of itinerating village libraries. The original capital for buying the books would be furnished by the Union, obtained mostly from gentlemen in the localities to be benefited, and the subscription of the readers to be at such a rate as would pay the entire expenses of management, and replace the books as they became worn out. The books should be removed at short and regular periods from village to village, and thus they would preserve the constant stimulus of novelty. The plan of itinerating libraries has been tried in Scotland very extensively, and in Cumberland also in connection with the Northern Union of Mechanics' Institutes, and it is being brought into operation in the Yorkshire Union of Mechanics' Institutes.[68]

The Report of the Parliamentary Committee on Public Libraries says,—

"It is the opinion of this Committee, that much of the future character of our agricultural population,

[68] See Appendix E.

social, moral, and religious, may depend on the extension and due formation of village libraries. In so important an object it is alike the duty of the landed proprietor and of the parochial clergy to assist. By such means the frivolous or unprincipled books which now circulate among our rural population[69] may be replaced by sound, healthy, and genuinely English literature. The people may be taught many lessons which concern their material, as well as their moral and religious welfare. The cleanliness and ventilation of their dwellings, habits of providence, of temperance, a taste for something better than mere animal enjoyment, may be instilled into them through the instrumentality of well-chosen books."[70]

It is clear that if some body superintending the general interests of adult education do not undertake the movement of such Institutes, no one else will, or can. The individual Institutes are too weak to act with much effect on the surrounding district, though doubtless many of them could do more than they do, by establishing small branch Institutes. Speaking on behalf of itinerating libraries above referred to, Mr. Edward Baines observes of the inhabitants of our villages,—

"For them no hall of philosophical society, or even of mechanics' institution, opens its doors; for them no well-stored museum spreads its wonders; for them no public library presents its shelves 'rich with the spoils of time;' to them no lecturer, noble or simple, unfolds the fruits of his life of study; to them no reading-room, or news-room, offers the attractive news of the day, mixed up with high discussion, with the discoveries and inventions of science, and tit-bits of literature and

69 *No* books rather than *frivolous* books, is the rule of village life. Of the two evils the last is the least.

70 Report from the Select Committee on Public Libraries, page 11.

poetry: such intellectual lights shine not in their firmament, —

> But clouds instead, and ever-during dark
> Surrounds them ;"

except, indeed, where the blaze of the public-house fire shines upon the beer-blurred newspaper, and the frequenters imbibe together the stimulants of politics and Sir John Barleycorn, till the latter asserts his easy supremacy, and muddles or inflames his rustic votaries.

" Such is notoriously the condition of thousands of small villages in this country, not indeed wholly out of the reach of our cheaper periodical literature, but cut off by the 'taxes on knowledge' from the luxury of a newspaper at their own firesides, and without any public means of improving their minds. Can we wonder that so many of our young men and women, taken at too early an age from school, forget the little they have learnt there, before they come to marry, and then sign the register with the mark which proves how little qualified they are to fulfil the intellectual duties of parents ?"[71]

We have dwelt on the subject of extending the agencies for adult instruction by means of a Central Union, because we feel that its importance has not been sufficiently appreciated. Whatever subdivisions it might be found desirable to introduce by means of County and Sub-Unions, a National Union with its seat in London is essential, for there are objects which no body out of London could so well accomplish, and there are some aids that the Union might render to *all* Institutes, which it would be a loss of labour to provide for one district merely. Amongst the objects which would devolve upon such a National Union as we propose, would be the securing of adequate attention to the welfare of Mechanics' Institutes on the part of the Legislature. A

[71] Leeds Mercury, December 14th 1852.

body in London representing the interests of a vast confederacy of Institutes would deserve, and naturally command, an influence to which no Provincial Union or isolated Institute could aspire. The Council of the National Union would be able to furnish information to the members of either House of Parliament at the time it was wanted, to organise public opinion on any question of importance (connected with the cause of adult education), and to get expressions of that opinion by means of petitions, meetings, &c. Of the importance of some such body to act for the Institutes, two illustrations suggest themselves, in which questions of great urgency to Mechanics' Institutes are in abeyance, simply for want of power on the part of the Institutes to bring their just claims before the Legislature.

One of these is, the power to protect their property, and punish fraud and dishonesty. In some places Institutions have had large portions of their property boldly taken away by members who had only subscribed a few shillings. Other cases are known to us, in which the Institutions having declined down to a very few members, these have divided the property among themselves, consisting of large quantities of valuable books given to the Institute on public grounds. An instance was recently named in the Journal of the Society of Arts. The writer says, "We have been great losers by the non-enrolment of the Mechanics' Institution, having lost in 1850 a library containing upwards of 2000 volumes, and other property which had cost more than 400*l*., through a difference existing among the members, and upon which difference the magistrates could not arbitrate, simply through the society being an illegal one. The result was a split between the members, about 150 seizing the whole property, and the remaining 600 members being left without anything. They consequently established our present Institution;

and the old one (the Working Man's Institution), after struggling for some time, finally disposed of the greater portion of the property for about 12*l*., and ceased to exist. This difference and sacrifice of public property was occasioned through a small portion of the members wishing to introduce works of an objectionable tendency into the library." [72] The want of legal protection has been sometimes an obstacle to the erection of suitable buildings; and unless legislative protection be extended to the property of these societies, we anticipate that the instances of dishonesty to these Institutes will be multiplied.

The Committee of the Yorkshire Union of Mechanics' Institutes thus state the difficulties under which the Institutes labour in the protection of their property:—

"Your Committee have, during the past year, carefully reconsidered the very important subject of investing the Institutes with efficient powers for self-regulation and security of property. The preliminary question is, whether that object can be attained by trust-deed alone, or will require the aid of the legislature? The difficulties of a trust-deed, unaided by legislative sanction, are very serious. They apply in some measure to the buildings of an Institution, but in a much greater degree to its books and moveable property. These, being either given to the members or bought with their money, will become their joint property, except so far as the rules of the Institution may affect or abridge their rights. Unless the rules are framed so as to exclude the members from all proprietary right whatever, and leaving them only a revocable privilege of qualified enjoyment, they are part-owners, and the part-owner of a book or other chattel is not amenable for the misappropriation of it to the criminal law, or (except where specially provided by

[72] Society of Arts Journal, No. 9. page 104, January 21st 1853.

the legislature) to any summary jurisdiction. No trust-deeds or rules which should stop short of absolute exclusion of members from proprietary right, will remove the difficulty, because all deeds and rules stopping short of that point are, in their nature, only contracts between the part-owners of a chattel, by which each binds himself to certain limits on the exercise of his separate rights of ownership, for the general benefit of his co-owners and himself, and no contentious jurisdiction, either criminal or civil, contrary to the usual course of law, can be created by contracts. The alternative, therefore, is, between leaving the books and moveable property to such protection as Courts of Equity or Common Law (including County Courts) may be able to afford, which might often prove inadequate; or framing the trust-deeds, or rules, so as to invest the trustees of the Institution with all the powers of absolute legal ownership over its books and moveable property, and leave to the members merely a revocable privilege of using them. If the trustees were a changing body, a new trust-deed would be necessary upon every change; and if a permanent one, they could not retain the management of an Institution in their own hands without violating the essential principles of self-government. They must, therefore, either be made responsible for the acts of a fluctuating Committee of Management, to which few trustees would consent, or be left irresponsible, which, if they are at the same time to be invested with powers of absolute legal ownership over the books and moveable property, would leave the members at their mercy. To these difficulties, which are inseparable from any attempt to regulate Institutions, whether existing or future, by trust-deed alone, must be added others applying to most, if not all, existing Institutions.

"Interests already subsist in the property of such Institutions which it would be difficult, and may sometimes be found impossible, to trace and define, and several of which, if traced and defined, would be found vested in married females, minors, or others, either nwilling or under legal disability to transfer them to trustees. In all such cases, the title of the trustees would, without legislative assistance, be imperfect; the imperfection might lead to future litigation, and, in the case of buildings or real property, would render it difficult to obtain a loan on mortgage. These, and other difficulties, appeared to your Committee so great as to render further advice necessary, and they accordingly consulted Robert Hall, Esq., the Recorder of Doncaster, who concludes an elaborate opinion on the whole subject, by the following sentence: 'I consider that the assistance of the Legislature is necessary to secure any approximation to uniformity of organisation, and, at least as regards most existing Institutions, to have the power of suing or prosecuting members, and to give power of self-regulation and modification on many points, such as the ultimate application of the funds, without having recourse to the Court of Chancery.' "[73]

To meet these difficulties, the Union of Institutes, in connection with the Society of Arts, in their Journal of Feb. 4th, 1853, propose to prepare a Bill for the sanction of Parliament, which will contain a "clause declaring that the Acts cited in the margin, being the 'School Sites Acts' now in force, shall be applicable in all respects as fully and completely to Institutions, as if they were the Schools originally contemplated in those Acts.

4 & 5 Vict. c. 28.
7 & 8 Vict. c. 37.
12 & 13 Vict. c. 49.
13 & 14 Vict. c. 28.
14 & 15 Vict. c. 24.

"If such a clause should become law, nearly all the restrictions and expensive processes which in this country impede the transfer of real property, and which

[73] Yorkshire Union Report for 1852.

in numerous cases absolutely prevent the due conveyance of the sites of Institutes, would become inoperative against the parties to a conveyance of land or buildings for an Institute. Such property might then be granted, conveyed, or enfranchised for such an object by a simple and inexpensive form, by any person beneficially interested, and being seized in fee simple, fee tail, or for life, by any lord or lady of a manor in respect of common land, by the officers of the Duchies of Cornwall and Lancaster, by clergymen in respect of glebe, by any person equitably entitled to but not holding the legal estate in land, by any infant or lunatic through his guardian or committee, by any justices of the peace, corporations, trustees, or commissioners for public, ecclesiastical, parochial, charitable, or other purpose. Moreover, the legal estates in the Institutes might be vested in any corporate body or bodies, sole or aggregate, lay or ecclesiastical, without licence to hold land in mortmain, without renewal of deeds, and without risk of an expiry of trusts. An efficacious and cheap remedy would be provided against any unlawful "holding over" of the premises on the part of any resident officer. The death of a grantor within twelve months would not invalidate a grant. The conveyance of copyhold by the lord and by the tenant in one deed, would vest the freehold in the grantee without surrender or admittance in the lord's court. Conveyances might be made to trustees and to their successors in office."

So far as to real property. With respect to the misappropriation of the personal property they say, "this might easily be remedied by well-conceived enactments; and secretaries, collectors, or other functionaries (query members) misappropriating the funds or other property of an Institute, might be declared guilty of a misdemeanour, in accordance with the precedent of the Savings Bank Act, 7 & 8 Vict. c. 83."

Another point on which the assistance of the Legislature is needed, is the exemption of such societies from local rates and general taxation. In this instance, the Legislature need only be called upon to re-affirm, and apply its own expressed intentions. By the Act 6 & 7 Vict. c. 36, the lands and buildings occupied by scientific and literary societies were to be exempt from county, borough, parochial, and other local rates.[74] It is no very great boon to the cause of national education, yet good as an acknowledgment of the principle; and in the deplorable financial condition of these Institutes, even the small sum that would be demanded by the rate-collector is of great importance. If the Legislature extended adequate assistance to the Institutes, we would rather such an exemption were done away with altogether. But even this concession is in danger from some defect in the Act, and a few decisions. Indeed, the Institutes that enjoy exemption are more indebted to the forbearance of those who levy the rates, and of the magistrates, than to the protection of the Act. A vigorous effort was made in 1849 to get a more definite act, but failed, owing, we believe, to accidental circumstances. There was no public body in London to *renew* the attempt in the next session, and the support given by the Institutes to the movement was not such as to tempt the promoters of it to persistent action.

The question whether the Institutes shall become the depositories of a selection of the reports and papers printed from time to time by order of the House of Commons, is now waiting the decision of a committee of that House. But that this point is being dealt with is owing to the motion of a private member (Mr. Tufnell) rather than to any action on the part of the Institutes[75], is another confirmation of our view.

[74] Passed 28th July, 1843.

[75] A petition, praying for the grant of these papers, was adopted at the last conference of delegates to the Yorkshire Union Meeting, 1852. Another has been drawn up by the Society of Arts, and circulated among the Institutes.

There are other illustrations of the advantages of a Central Union. For example, a system of keeping the accounts of Mechanics' Institutes in the best and simplest form is much to be desired. In many Institutions, especially small ones, the accounts are kept, if it may be called keeping at all, in the most wretched manner. The entry of the books from the library to the members, and the checking them off when returned, is a simple operation, yet one performed in an endless variety of ways. Yet there must be a *best* way, both of keeping the accounts, and recording the issue and return of books.

It is not meant by this that there is one plan which would suit alike the large town and the village Institutes. There would probably be required three or even four forms of book-keeping adapted to the various classes of Institutes. The National Union would render most important services by devising some clear and uniform method, and making its principles known to every Institute. It might then be worth the while of a respectable account-book maker to keep complete sets of the books on hand, so that they could be readily obtained as wanted, and at a much lower cost when prepared on a large scale.

The direct benefit would not be the only one. The adoption of a uniform principle of keeping the accounts would assist the Institutes to furnish those comparative statistics which are of the greatest value in judging of existing modes of management, and guiding to future improvements. The reports of the Institutes to the Union fail in one of their chief advantages, if they do not each furnish information on the same points. It becomes impossible either to ascertain the total amount of any one agency embodied in the Institutes, or the relative influence of any causes deduced from comparisons of their effects.

The " Rules for Mechanics' Institutes " in the Manual

of the Society for the Diffusion of Useful Knowledge, contain many valuable suggestions as to the modes of conducting the business of an Institute, but are too cumbersome. A copy of them curtailed and adapted to present wants, would be of great value, especially in the formation of new Institutions.

A catalogue of books suitable for Mechanics' Institutes is much wanted. It might serve as a model of the classification of the works, and should name the nett price and the publisher of each work. It should include also those books, many of them of standard value, which are sure to be found on the shelves of the second-hand booksellers. A supplement should be issued annually, containing a list of the new works specially adapted to Mechanics' Institutes, which had been published during the year. Large numbers of the Committees, especially in the small towns and villages, never get to see the publishers' and booksellers' catalogues, and if they do, they know too little of the works to be able to form an opinion, so as to spend their funds to the best advantage.

The list of books issued by a National Union would be valuable, not merely as suggestive of works to be bought, but, if judiciously done, as a guide in the selection. If this proposed list came in the form of a classified catalogue, it might be made to indicate, under each division, what are the most important works in each branch of knowledge, thus ensuring a degree of completeness alike in the libraries of the small and of the larger Institutes.

Thus, if figures were adopted, 1 would indicate that the book was indispensable; 2, that it was desirable for a wider circle; 3, if a still larger selection was desired; and so on. The Yorkshire Union is about to issue such a catalogue; but as the Mechanics' Institutes in one county do not differ from those in another, which may have no Union, and as clear accounts, good rules, and a suggestive catalogue, are advantages that *all* Institutes should possess, the preparation of these things more properly devolves upon a National Union. Indeed, if such helps were prepared for the whole country, they might be done with a perfection not to be expected in those provided for a single county.

We will next consider those direct advantages which organisation might confer upon the individual societies, and, first in importance, come the lectures.

We have already stated the very small proportion of paid lectures taken by the Institutes, and the consequent failure of the Yorkshire Union for combined courses of lectures. The same remark applies to the other county unions wherever they have existed long enough for the novelty of such arrangements to pass away.[76] If Mechanics' Institutes are to remain in the same state they have been in for some years past, and if unions continue to have no funds other than those furnished by the societies in combination with them, the prospect of any advantage to Mechanics' Institutes in the way proposed is small indeed.

We trust those who have originated the Union of Mechanics' Institutes in connection with the Society of Arts, will remember this, lest they but repeat the failure of other unions; and without their plea of want of ex-

[76] Out of the 236 Institutes in connection with the Society of Arts, to each of which a schedule was sent, asking for information, to ascertain the subjects on which they were willing to have lectures, and the sums they were willing to give for the same, only 137 made returns; and of these not more than 83 expressed a wish to make them for the present season. The total number of lectures required was 306, and, while the lowest fee offered was 1*l.*, the highest was but 5*l.* 5*s.* to include travelling and other expenses: 30 were requested at fees not amounting to more than 40*s.* each. (Mr. Harry Chester's Report of the Institutes' Committee, Jan. 12th, 1853, in the Journal of the Society of Arts, No. 8.)

In the Northern Union, an arrangement was made with an eminent scientific lecturer of London to deliver twenty lectures, on consecutive evenings, at *one guinea* per lecture. "Liberal as these terms were, the committee found, with extreme regret, that only six engagements could be obtained, and these from societies lying so wide apart, that they were reluctantly compelled to abandon the project." (Report, 1852.)

perience. It is to be hoped, however, that the growth of intelligence, and the awakened attention of the nation and of the Government, to the necessities of industrial education, will so improve our Institutes, that it shall be in the power of each to secure complete courses of good lectures.

There are two methods of economising the expense of lectures. One is by reducing the payment to the lecturer himself. Under the impression that the engagements to be offered him by the unions will be numerous, and the excusable desire to tempt the committee to engage him,—perhaps, too, with that disregard of his pecuniary interests too characteristic of men engaged in scientific and literary vocations,—he often agrees to lecture for a sum, which, when his expenses are deducted, will scarcely leave the wages of unskilled labour. Of all false economies, this is the most pernicious, and (shall we say) the most cruel. It tends to drive from the profession of lecturer every man of ability, who naturally seeks that remuneration in other departments which he cannot find in this. We knew an eminent lecturer who lately died in extreme poverty, as well he might, who agreed to give lectures to Institutions, and to pay his travelling expenses and carriage of apparatus, all for the sum of 25*s.* per lecture. And sums not very much larger than this are frequently paid to able professional lecturers. Unions in future must take care that whatever the terms on which lecturers are engaged, they shall at least have proper payment for the talent employed.

The other method of economising the cost of lectures, is that of arranging the engagements of the lecturer. It saves him much time and trouble, and by combining his engagements in topographical order, and at convenient periods, travelling expenses and the cost of carriage of apparatus are saved. All that can be saved in this way is true economy.

There is little doubt that a Union with its centre in London could afford valuable aid to both lecturers and Institutes. The large majority of professional leeturers reside in London, where the Secretary of the Union would be at hand to furnish all information the lecturer might desire, such as the names and localities of the provincial Institutes; the subjects on which lectures are wanted; the distances and expenses of travelling, and of carriage of apparatus. It is obvious that such information had better be accurately ascertained and registered once for all, than that every lecturer should have the information to ferret out for himself. It would be useful, even when no engagements were arranged through the medium of the Union. Whether engagements for lectures were made through the Union or not, a national centre would be essential, since a single county, however large, contains but few Institutes capable of contracting for paid lectures. Railways have brought the opposite ends of the kingdom nearer together than two towns in the same county were a few years ago. Engagements entered into through the recommendation of the central committee would afford a guarantee of the character and ability of the lecturer, through ignorance of which local committees have often seriously suffered.

If a national organisation of the Institutes were perfected to the utmost, we do not think it could alone bring the lecturing system into the highest state of efficiency. We have seen the tendency of the Institutes to diminish the scientific and practical lecturers, to introduce those of a lighter class, because, whatever else is done, the directors must make it *pay*. If this is the case with the largest and most prosperous Institutes, what can we expect from the others? In small towns, the centres of agricultural industry, no Institution can pay for lectures. Yet how valuable it would be if they could have only one course of lectures in a season on agricultural chemistry or other cognate subject. In the mining districts, how useful some lectures on the nature of the gases from which the miner suffers, and the means which science suggests for his protection. Speaking on this subject, Sir Henry T. De la Beche observes:—"Much good may no doubt arise from the appointment of inspectors of collieries in the different districts in this country; but the more effective saving of life from colliery explosions must be looked for in the instruction generally of the coal miners themselves. The amount of mischief arising from the fool-hardiness of ignorance in our collieries can only be credited by those who are compelled to employ men with a want of education they deplore, or who have in discharge of duties visited coal mines after fearful and desolating explosions."[77]

In all towns, how many scientific subjects are there capable of popular elucidation, of which even a slight knowledge would be of the highest value to the community. Whatever the grand Industrial University, yet in embryo, is destined to accomplish, and no one regards this magnificent conception more hopefully than ourselves,— it will not fulfil its greatest objects unless its teachers and professors carry the knowledge there acquired to the remotest towns and villages of our country. And they can only do this effectually, when, on the one hand, they are properly paid for their labour, and, on the other, are placed under the direction of a body who know the local wants, can point out to each lecturer where his peculiar information will be most valuable, and offer to him the means of coming in contact with the local committees. The Institutes thus provided with competent teachers and lecturers, would become branch colleges for the carrying out of the great objects of the Industrial University, while their own powers of self-

[77] Lectures on the Great Exhibition; "Mining, Quarrying, and Metallurgical Processes and Products," p. 46.

government and self-development would be free from interference. The Central Union, therefore, should occupy a prominent place in the great Industrial University, and it ought to have the power (under proper restrictions) of distributing the services of competent lecturers wherever they might be needed. Without supplying all that is wanted, it would at least serve as a commencement towards meeting our great deficiencies.

The Government, at the recommendation of a Parliamentary Committee, in 1836, enabled the Dublin Society[78] to pay lecturers to visit the Institutes in Ireland, and their visits were attended, says Mr. Wyse, "with very great success." And if this was the case in a country in which almost every thing done by Government was opposed by bigotry, jealousy, and suspicion,— where that which would be deemed beneficent in any other place on the broad earth was turned into a plague and a curse,—we are warranted in believing that in the improved tone of public feeling in this country, such help would be still more advantageous, especially if wielded by those most intimate with the wants and necessities of these Institutes.

The plan of the Yorkshire Union of Mechanics' Institutes in sending a paid agent to the branches, contains the germ of that plan which a National Union should adopt in the management of such a scheme as we propose. If the funds could be obtained from the Government—and we have little hope of them from any other source—a large amount of systematic instruction in practical science might be conveyed. To produce anything like a satisfactory result, every Institute ought to have at least one good course of lectures in a season, primarily on subjects connected with the trade, manufactures, and staple occupation of the district. If possible, there should be class examinations in connection

[78] The locality visited had to defray a small portion of the expenses.

with these lectures; and these class examinations would be greatly facilitated by the lecturer furnishing his hearers with a carefully prepared syllabus of the heads of his lecture. From time to time, subjects might be taken more remotely related to the former, or topics of general and high importance to the working classes. The size of the district visited at one time, should not be greater than sufficient to give the proper treatment of the subject at each. Suppose four lectures were given per week—and no one ought to be expected to give more—four places would be selected lying near to each other, and one lecture be delivered at each place in regular succession on the like day of the week. When the lecturer had finished his course, he should go to the adjoining locality and proceed over the same course in four other Institutes, and by the end of the lecture season he would have gone through the whole of his district. The following winter he might visit another district. In summer he would have leisure to prepare his lectures.

If the lectures are arranged to be delivered in the Institutes according to their geographical position,—and no other plan is so economical of time, labour, and money,—the arrangement of the order in which the places are visited *must rest with the managers of the Union, not with the committee of the Institute.* The utmost power that can be allowed them, is the negative one of declining any course of lectures. If the dates of the special lectures were communicated in ample time to every Institute intended to be visited, they could have no ground of complaint, for they might adopt their other arrangements accordingly.

Such a plan would require a very much larger staff of lecturers than one lecturer to 120 Institutes, as in the Yorkshire Union. There would not be a great difficulty in finding, even now, able men versed in their special subjects, and well able to give lectures, if they could be secured a proper remuneration. A few of the largest Institutes could contribute towards the expense, though they could not defray it entirely. But in the large majority of Institutes, they could do nothing towards it. They can hardly maintain themselves, and any addition to their expenses would quite swamp them.

We do not recommend above one course in a season to be supplied in this way. There is a large fund of lecture talent which, although little estimated by those who are not familiar with the economy of these Institutes, requires but organisation to render it very valuable. Gratuitous lectures, delivered by persons residing in the locality of the Institute, are now more than four times more numerous than the paid ones, and though we would gladly see this proportion in some degree changed in favour of the latter, the gratuitous lectures neither should nor can be dispensed with. Experience convinces us that, in small towns and villages, a familiar lecture by an amateur pleases better than one by a scientific man, unless the latter possesses the rare qualification of conveying his information in the simplest manner. Nor are our educational agencies so perfect that we can afford to despise help from any quarter. In the class of those able and willing thus to minister to the amusement and instruction of their fellow men, at no slight cost of study, there exists an enormous power for the diffusion of knowledge. Nearly every village contains its minister of religion, its medical man, its lawyer, and its schoolmaster, capable of giving general information on topics of vital importance to the welfare of the community, such as moral and social duties, the laws and conditions of health and disease, the nature and origin of our laws and institutions. Let them exert their powers, and they will awaken the minds of those around them to seek for further information. Then, again, almost all well-informed persons have some subject of special interest to themselves, with which they could pleasantly and profitably engage the attention of others for an hour. The committee of every Institute should lay under contribution all the knowledge and talent around them.[79] To carry out this object, small districts or sub-unions of ten or twelve Institutes might be formed. Let Institutes notify, either to a meeting of delegates from each Institute in the district, or to the secretary of the County Union, the names of all parties willing or likely to give lectures within the district. The districts must not be large, nor embrace widely scattered Institutes, for that would raise an obstacle to obtaining lectures. A list of these, containing the address of the person willing to lecture, the subject, time, and number of lectures suitable to him, should be prepared and issued to each Institute in time to enable the committee to make up their list of lectures for the winter. The Institute would of course have to pay the travelling expenses and carriage of apparatus (if any). This plan was tried in the Yorkshire Union during the present winter, but for want of a division of the county into smaller districts, and also from the Institutes not being sufficiently alive to the advantages of the plan, its success was not what it might have been. However, no less than sixty-two persons responded to the invitation of the secretary to offer lectures, the list was published in the Union Report, and we know Institutes which were enabled to fill up their list of lectures for the winter solely by this aid. Those lecturers who fail to attract or instruct their audiences, ceasing to be invited, will be weeded out, while the success of others will encourage the development of real talent.

To assist this class of lecturers, a most excellent plan has been originated by the Working Man's Educational Union. They have expended very large sums in preparing first-rate coloured diagrams, printed on cotton,

79 Vide Yorkshire Union Report, 1858, page 15.

which are sold at an exceedingly low price. Complete sets of diagrams on the Antiquities of Nineveh, on Astronomy, Physiology, Mechanics, the Telescope, Habitations and Dwellings of Scripture, Pagan Rites, &c., have already been issued. The diagrams are each twelve square feet in area, printed on cloth, adapted for distant inspection, coloured for candle-light, and are both durable and very portable. It has also issued a very excellent little manual, entitled "Practical Hints to Unpractised Lecturers to the Working Classes."[80] The diagrams are well done, and will much improve the effect and increase the attractions of lectures, and help to multiply the number of those who are wishful to aid the public in the work of self-instruction. Pictorial illustration is one of the readiest ways of reaching the people, and it would have a most advantageous educational influence, if this and other plans of the Working Men's Educational Union could be much extended. There are many professional men who would be willing to give lectures, if only the diagrams, or the apparatus needful for illustrating them, were readily accessible. The Union might charge a small sum for the loan of the apparatus or the diagrams, to repay the outlay upon them.

Skeletons of lectures, and a stock of good manuscript lectures, if not of much, are of some value, and a collection might easily be made by the Union. The Yorkshire Union possesses upwards of 100 manuscript lectures, and though many of them have been read several times, which will naturally diminish the demand for them, the circulation of them last year was thirty-eight.

We have discussed the question of a Union of Institutes on its own merits, without reference to the Union formed by the Society of Arts last year, but we have no hesitation in saying, that *that* Union ought to undertake

[80] F. Baron, 43 Skinner Street, Snow Hill.

the duties here assigned it. Even if it had not nobly occupied the ground, there exists no other body to occupy it, or to initiate a national Union of Institutes. It entertains a sense of the important task it has undertaken, and if it has not yet achieved much for the Institutions in union with it, this arises partly from the shortness of its existence, and partly because no Union can perform much whose activity is contingent solely upon the contributions derived from the respective Institutes. What it has done has been in the right direction. Its connection with the Society of Arts we regard as a peculiarly advantageous feature. The Society of Arts may be considered as the reservoir of industrial knowledge, and the Union as the machinery for its distribution. The production of a good box of colours and a case of instruments at a price which would bring them within the reach of the poorest, was a desideratum. We do not see why the department of Practical Art, which is now issuing drawing copies of models at half price, should not co-operate with the Union, and offer through it the same advantages to Mechanics' Institutes. Some of them have already received the Elementary Drawing Book, but not one Institute in a score is aware that it might obtain that book. Atlases, maps, models, diagrams, and other appliances, might be obtained cheaper by a central Union purchasing them wholesale for distribution among the Institutes, and where Institutes could not readily get supplied with books, the Union might act as agent for the purchase of them.

We have already spoken of the value of occasional exhibitions of works of art, machinery, and specimens of natural objects. The Union might assist the object in two ways. It might by means of the inventions rewarded by the Society of Arts, and the donations given to it for that purpose, form a valuable nucleus for such exhibitions, to which, of course, must be added the contributions of the locality benefited by the exhibition. There are numerous persons who would be willing to lend paintings and objects of *vertù* in the place to be benefited thereby, especially in conjunction with such contributions as the Society of Arts could make if they once thoroughly undertook the task. The Union could also assist, not only by furnishing contributions, but also by organising skill to bring them together. In small towns where such exhibitions are very desirable, there are few, often none, who would know how to set about "getting up an exhibition;" they do not know their own resources until some one points them out. A visit by some competent person from the Central Union to the local Committee to confer with them, not merely to ascertain how far the Union could co-operate with them, but to initiate the process of formation, would be found essential.

The formation of local museums is an object of great importance, and one to which the Union in connection with the Society of Arts has already given prominence. The word "Museum" is apt to suggest something like the place of business of Shakspeare's Apothecary:—

> "In his needy shop
> A tortoise hung, an alligator stuffed,
> And other skins of ill-shaped fishes."

The Journal of the Society of Arts has very justly defined what is meant by a museum adapted for the purposes of Instruction, as distinguished from one to make country people stare away an idle hour when on a holiday visit to a neighbouring town. "A museum, properly considered, is not a collection of curiosities, antiquities, and artistic works, grouped together in glass cases, in a species of native confusion; but if it deserves its name, is a place in which instruction is to be gained, and consequently in which order, arrangement, and method is evident throughout. Arrangement in a museum is of the very first consequence; without it the specimens, however good, are isolated, and tend only to confuse; whilst when well arranged, and according to some kind of order, they at once become instructive and suggestive; so that even a careless observer cannot fail to learn something from their examination. Collections may be formed illustrative of various subjects and for many different purposes; they may be made to illustrate the several branches of natural science, such as geology, mineralogy, botany, zoology, entomology, &c.; they may be formed to illustrate the mechanical arts and manufactures; they may be historical, and designed to show the progressive development of the human race, or ethnological, illustrating the habits and customs of particular people. Excellent artistic collections too may be made, in which beautiful forms and appropriate combinations of colour are shown so as insensibly to educate the eye to the appreciation of the true principles of taste; but in these and in all similar cases the collections lose their chief value if they are not well arranged: the systematic and consecutive arrangement constituting an essential feature in all really instructive museums. A geological collection, for example, in which specimens of the various strata of the earth are arranged in the same order as that in which they naturally occur, and each one accompanied by its own peculiar organic remains, and the mineral productions or metallic ores occurring in it, is highly instructive; but if we add to it good geological maps, and illustrations of the uses in the arts to which those ores and stones are applied, its value is very much increased." Its nature and relations to Mechanics' Institutes, and the way in which the Society of Arts' Union proposes it should be carried out, are thus explained in the circular of the secretary, Mr. Solly.

"There are many places in which from situation or the circumstances of trade, specimens of various kinds, which in other places are rare or difficult to obtain, may be had with very little trouble or cost. Almost every town is noted for some staple production or manufacture, and it would of course be easy to form a small collection of specimens in illustration of such manufacture. In the mining districts it would be easy to collect specimens in illustration of the various metallurgical arts; and in every place, geological, botanical, or entomological collections may be formed, which, taken by themselves, are unquestionably interesting and instructive, but the value of which is greatly increased when they are brought together, and so arranged that the productions of different localities may be compared and contrasted.

"In every place, however, it would be far less trouble and expense to form twenty similar small local collections of the productions or manufactures of the neighbourhood, than it would to collect as many separate collections from different places; and consequently, a systematic interchange of local collections would necessarily save time and trouble, and lead to the benefit of all parties.

"The first step obviously is, to ascertain in how far the Institutions themselves would approve of such a plan; and secondly, whether they would be willing to co-operate with the Society of Arts in forming collections of the manufactures or productions of their own neighbourhoods, for the purposes of being exchanged with those of other places. I shall be glad to hear from you on the subject, if any members of your Society are willing to lend their aid and assistance in carrying out the proposed plan." [81]

We do not know what response was made to this excellent proposal, beyond the fact that upwards of seventy replied, all more or less favourable to the plan; but from what we know of the difficulties under which these Institutes are carried on, and the duties of their overworked and mostly unpaid officials, we venture to

[81] July 19. 1852.

predict that the result will be *nil;* until either the efficiency of the local Institutes is materially increased, or a visit from an active agent has shown to the local committees what is wanted, how it is to be done, and the benefit that will accrue.

The American Lyceums have shown what can be done in this way, merely by the application of the exertions of the members of the Town Lyceums. Mr. Wyse states, that in this way the various Lyceums were provided, at a very small cost, with excellent elementary museums, and the "systematic interchange of local collections" proposed by the Secretary of the Society of Arts, was there effected, by the establishment of a general deposit and distributing office at New York, under the direction of the national department of the Institution. "Thousands of children of not more than eight or ten years old now know more of geology, mineralogy, botany, statistical facts, &c. &c.,—in fine, of what immediately concern their daily interests and occupations,—than was probably known thirty years ago by any five individuals in the United States. Indeed, so universally, and to such excellent profit is the task diffused, that in some sections of the country the majority of the school-houses are furnished with collections procured by the children themselves."[81a]

Another thing which has often been an object of desire to those who would improve our Mechanics Institutes, is an institutional periodical devoted to their interests. This is obviously a task devolving upon an union, and the Society of Arts have in their little *Journal* wisely endeavoured to carry it out. For making our Institutes known and appreciated outside of their own circle, we must of course trust to the general newspaper, and to periodical publications An Institute having the power to keep its doings before the public in this way, acts very unwisely in

81a See Appendix F.

neglecting the opportunity. There is, however, a large amount of special information which requires a special journal for its collection and diffusion. Opportunities for the communication of all facts and events in which such Institutes are interested, and for discussing practical suggestions, are thus afforded. To effect much good a large circulation should be secured. Out of the great number enjoying the benefits of Mechanics' Institutes, a tolerable circulation should be obtained, but will not for the present *Journal*, without a considerable reduction in the price[82], which now excludes all but the wealthy from purchasing it. For a periodical devoted to their interests we think that the Institutes ought to constitute themselves special agents. They might each guarantee to take a certain number of copies at a reduced price.[83] Thus it would be brought under the attention of their members, nine-tenths of whom will otherwise never even know of its existence.

Such a periodical would not supersede, but rather form the material for, an annual Report of the condition and prospects of the Institutions, which should embody whatever was of permanent value in the records. Statistics furnished upon an organized plan, from a large number of Institutes, would furnish most useful data for further improvement. The Report might contain the yearly list of books,valuable for the libraries, with such brief notices of the contents of each work as would enable the local committee to judge of its utility.

The arrangement for the interchange of privileges between the Institutes is another duty devolving upon the Union. When the member of an Institute is visiting another town, the production of his card of

[82] The price is 3*d.*, and stamped 4*d.*, being as much as the whole subscription paid for membership in the majority of Institutes. To members of the Society of Arts it is issued gratis.

[83] This would save the stamp, as the Institutes might get them in their parcels.

membership should be sufficient, if his admission is required but for two or three days. When the admission is required for a longer period, a travelling card issued by the Union, and distributed to all the Institutes permitting the interchange of privileges, would be the readiest mode of carrying out the system. Some limitations must, however, be permitted to the Institutes, to prevent abuse. It has been found that persons (and even some well-off in circumstances) residing in the neighbourhood of large towns, have joined a village Institute outside, to enable them to visit the large Institute of the town on market days, thus substituting 1*d.* per week subscription for one, three, or four times larger.

The importance of examinations and certificates of proficiency has already been insisted on. If the Union were to appoint a board of examiners, who should hold periodical examinations, it would meet the case of Institutes situated in the smaller towns, and which might experience some difficulty in finding persons competent to the task; even larger Institutes would probably be glad to have the services of such examiners if judiciously selected, from the confidence which their certificates of proficiency would give.

The recommendation of teachers for the classes and day schools of Mechanics' Institutes, the pointing out of improved modes of tuition, the recommending of new and good apparatus for teaching; of furniture for schools and class rooms,—these are points that but indicate the extensive field of usefulness in which an efficient and active central body might labour. But for a central body to reap either the advantages to which we have called attention, or any others which augmented experience may show to be possible, adequate means must be placed at its disposal. In a well organised association the whole becomes not merely equal to, but greater than, the parts. Now to expect from any combination a result disproportionate to the contribution made to it, will merely lead to disappointment. Either Institutes must contribute more to such Unions, or expect less from them. We do not mean contributions in funds merely, but in sympathy, and participation in common objects. So little sensible are the Institutes generally of the advantages of such Unions, or perhaps it would be more just to say, so badly are they themselves managed, that they frequently neglect to reply to the letters from the Central Committee. What would a merchant think, or how could business be carried on, if such neglect should take place in commercial transactions? No doubt the (too often unpaid) Secretary of the Institute finds enough demand upon his little leisure for the ordinary purposes of the Institute; perhaps too he has a dilatory Committee to consult before he can reply, and so he omits altogether.[84] The Secretary of the Union, also unpaid, cannot spare time for other correspondence than that of a printed circular; hence no intimate knowledge can spring up between the central body and the local Institute. All this is lamentable, and would not be tolerated an instant if the central body and the local Institutes were private persons engaged on matters of *£ s. d.* And is it to be supposed that because the objects aimed at are of a more elevated character, and for the public benefit, that the ordinary rules of business can be disregarded? We may be assured that no association will succeed unless it can contrive to infuse the same energy, the same skill, order, and punctuality, into the details of business, which characterise well-managed private establishments. It may be great at annual speech-makings, but any Society, or any Union

[84] The Secretary of the Northern Union lately addressed 81 Institutes, and received answers from 17. His application to them was to join the Union at a reduced rate of subscription. We could furnish a score of similar instances.

of Societies, which does not contrive to confer solid advantages on its constituents, is at the mercy of every accident, and will speedily be added to the list of the many well-meant, but ephemeral organisations which the last few years have witnessed.

We have thus endeavoured to trace the nature and causes of the deficiencies which our Institutes for Adult Instruction exhibit, to point out the objects at which they should aim, and the means by which they are to be secured. If by the means suggested, these Institutes could be placed in a position of solvency and efficiency, the next ten years will suffice to show greater results in the improved intellectual condition of the people of this country than has been achieved in the last thirty years, great as the progress has been in that time. Nothing would more effectually disarm the hostility, secret or avowed, of the opponents of popular education, than a recognition of their objects by the State, in the way recommended. It would also tend to attract the highest order of talent, both literary and scientific, to their lecture halls, and season the mediocrity which prevails there. Superior lectures would bring the middle ranks, superior class instruction would draw the operatives to the Institution, and thus a common ground whereon they could meet would be secured, and a friendlier, healthier feeling between the employer and the employed be promoted. The domain of political liberty is enlarging; if we would use it aright, if we would guard against fatal reactions, we must multiply intelligence in at least an equal degree. The right of free inquiry, the obligation to seek for truth, are becoming generally acknowledged, and acted upon. Without education, this right is but ridiculous presumption, liable to lead to all kinds of absurdities. We have invited the world to free competition,—the competition of intelligence,—we stake our industrial pre-eminence on the issue. If we fail to keep up our superiority, it will be our fault and our shame; the lesson of 1851 will for us have been in vain. Our Institutes are not what they ought to be, what they might be; but we have this satisfactory thought — that there exists a remedy, that no insurmountable obstacle prevents their being equal to the great purposes they have to fulfil. Let us not, through apathy or a contented self-conceit, fail in our part in the work of progress and civilisation; let us show ourselves worthy of the blessings we inherit, by transmitting them with increased power to our successors.

APPENDICES.

APPENDIX A. Page 3.

Extracts from Memorials addressed by Corporations and other Public Bodies to the Royal Commissioners for the Exhibition of the Industry of all Nations.

Birmingham.

Your Memorialists have long felt the necessity of some more extended system of practical and scientific education in England, which should place within the reach of the industrial classes a much higher standard of scientific attainments than they can now ever hope to possess without very ample means.

Your Memorialists are convinced that with greater facilities in elementary scientific education, intimately connected with, and always accompanied by, practical illustrations and manipulations, there would be found as much original genius and talent to develop in the people of this country as in those of the great continental states of Europe; and that such development would greatly facilitate the maintenance and extension of our manufactures and commerce.

The great and rapid strides which locomotion has taken on the Continent, and the constant international communication which is the result, have extended science and mechanical and artistical knowledge widely over those nations; and thus one vast school of arts and sciences exists, with its members in constant communication, from which this country is partly excluded from its geographical position.

Some of your Memorialists, in their late visit to Paris, have witnessed the advantages which the rising generation of manufacturers is there enjoying in their educational establishments; and although not favoured by the possession of such vast resources in raw materials, mineral wealth and fuel, as Great Britain has the blessing to enjoy, they have established such colleges as the conservatory of arts and manufactures, and the central school of arts and manufactures, which are especially destined for the instruction of manufacturers and artisans, either entirely free or at a low charge.

These central colleges under the charge of the State, and with most efficient and interesting museums attached, have ramifications extending over other important manufacturing districts of the country.

In such schools are the youth of France brought up, receiving, particularly in the provincial schools attached to the conservatory, and in the central school of arts, the highest standard of scientific instruction in connection with the arts, manufactures, and design, matured by practical illustrations and experience in manipulation, and a knowledge of the particular trade in which they are eventually to devote their professional talent as designers.

Numerous young men educated at these colleges of first-rate talent and practical experience pass examinations of very high standard, and receive diplomas, which are a passport for them to many parts of the continent as managers and directors of most important manufactories and establishments, and enabling them to find lucrative employment even in England.

From these sources have sprung some of the most eminent men of the age, enjoying rank, consideration, and wealth, derived from the systematic education which they receive there.

Your Memorialists admit with pleasure and gratitude that the government has already made a great step in advancing this object, by the establishment of Schools of Design, and the Museum of Practical Geology; but still the first are only partial in their advantages, and the latter only an isolated branch, which exerts but little immediate beneficial influence over the arts and manufactures generally.

Bristol.

Your Memorialists abstain from any details as to the benefits to be derived from the adoption of such an institution, and content themselves with merely suggesting, that, if any plan analogous to that above referred to should meet the approval and countenance of your honourable board, you will devise such means as will render it as diffusive as possible, and take measures that it shall become an institution not confined to one locality, but by means of provincial schools in connection with a Metropolitan Central College, pervading and receiving attention and encouragement in the great manufacturing and commercial cities of the empire, so that what is at this moment a just source of national pride may, in its ultimate results, prove a national blessing.

Halifax.

Your Memorialists, immediately identified with one of the most important branches of the fancy textile productions of this country, have long felt, in common with other manufacturing districts, the great disadvantages under which they labour from the lack of a more accomplished education amongst the operative classes of the united kingdom, in the higher departments of art and science. Your Memorialists therefore humbly submit that a more appropriate dedication of the surplus funds, nor one more directly in harmony with the original expressed intention of your Honourable Board, could hardly be adopted than that of founding on a national basis a scheme of education, calculated to remove the disadvantages already referred to, alike important to the prosperity and welfare of every class of the community. It is abundantly recognized to what extent institutions of this kind have been promoted by our continental neighbours, and were practical evidences of the important benefits resulting from such a course not otherwise supplied, the truly elegant productions of France, Italy and Germany, which grace their several departments in the Crystal Palace, would amply establish them.

Your Memorialists feel it unnecessary to enter upon the details of such a project, as they will be so much more ably dealt with by your Honourable Board. They would only add that, in their humble judgment, unless a grand institution were founded, in which facilities were given of combining practice with theory, so that the student might pursue the one in direct association with the other, a scheme of such a character would best answer its purposes, i made to embrace a series of local establishments, acting under and in concert with one central Institution, constituting in the whole a National College or

University of Arts and Industry, empowered to grant certificates or diplomas to students of proficiency and merit.

Hull.

Your Memorialists perceive that, unless a system of industrial education is extended to this country, so as to enable our manufacturers to apply increased science and skill to their manufactures, England cannot keep her position in the great industrial competition of all nations; a competition, which has for its effect the increase in value of skill and intelligence, as applied to the manufacture of that raw material, which, by the facilities of transport, is becoming decreased in price. Your Memorialists see, therefore, to themselves a great advantage in giving to manufacturers the means of acquiring a scientific knowledge of the principles of their industries, so that they may apply them with the best advantage to their respective wants.

Your Memorialists would therefore impress upon your Honourable Board the necessity of establishing a central College of Arts and Manufactures, in connection with provincial schools, having the same object in view. They have full reliance that the great practical skill and aptitude of application which is a marking feature of the character of our countrymen, will enable our manufacturers to use the knowledge which they will thus have an opportunity of acquiring for the best purposes of industry.

Your Memorialists would like to see, in connection with the Central Educational Institution, means for special international Exhibitions; as, for example, of silks in one part, pottery in another, and so on: and they believe that these might be made a source of profit which could be used in the extension of the scheme of industrial education.

Oldham.

Your Memorialists regret that there does not exist in this country any national institution devoted to instruction on a similar basis to the schools of Arts and Manufactures established in France and Belgium, which, by imparting to their students the knowledge of the principles on which all improvements must be founded, have contributed so largely to the development of manufacturing skill.

Your Memorialists would, therefore, solicit your Honourable Board to take into consideration, in the disposal of the surplus fund which may remain in your hands, the immediate advantage which would be likely to accrue to the manufacturers of this country by the establishment of a Central College of Arts and Manufactures in connection with provincial schools for the same object, which should include the existing Schools of Design. This institution to be empowered to make examinations and grant certificates to the more advanced students, and to promote, by these and similar means, the cultivation of increased knowledge in application of science to practical pursuits, which could not fail to exercise a beneficial influence on industrial progress.

Sheffield.

Your Memorialists fully recognise that the improvements in locomotion and in the applications of science are gradually rendering available to all countries the raw materials which formerly were the privilege of a few, and that in consequence, while the value of the raw material is becoming reduced as an element in manufacture, the value of skill and intelligence to its preparation as another element is constantly increasing.

Your Memorialists observe that other countries, less favoured with fuel and raw materials than our own, have recognised this fact as a principle of state, and have established Schools of Manufacture, including Schools of Design, not only at their capitals, but also throughout their provincial towns.

Your Memorialists recognise in such institutions a wise intention on the part of foreign governments to develop manufactures, by applying increased science, skill, and intelligence to their cultivation. They feel that in the increasing competition of the world it is necessary to join education to practice, and although they do not think that a practical education in industrial science can ever of itself make manufacturers, they are fully convinced that when the scientific principles of manufactures are more thoroughly understood by practical men, they will better be able to apply them with advantage in their respective industries, and to promote economy and improvements in manufacturing processes.

Your Memorialists have observed that Government has considered it desirable to establish a Government School of Mines, in connection with the Museum of Practical Geology, and they perceive in this a recognition on the part of the State of the want of practical education to a large branch of industry. But your Memorialists in vain look for a college devoted to the industrial pursuits which they themselves follow, or to those important textile manufactures carried on by the neighbouring manufacturing towns.

They consider that if these branch institutions and the Central College were united into one university of arts and manufactures, empowered to make examinations and grant certificates to those who showed sufficient knowledge, an impulse and position would be given to manufacturing science, which could not fail to be of benefit to the progress of industry.

Staffordshire Potteries.

Your Memorialists are confidently of opinion, that a more extended and practical system of scientific education is necessary in this country,—a system which should offer on readily available terms to the industrial classes of England a much higher standard of productive acquirements than they now possess, and that ample facilities for a sound elementary education, in intimate connection with, and accompanied by, practical illustrations, alone are wanting to develop in our artists and artizans as large an amount of genius and talent as is evidenced in the best productions of the great continental emporiums, and also that such a development would greatly tend to the increase of our manufactures and commerce.

They would therefore recommend that a central college of art and manufacture be established in London, and a museum connected with it. That provincial schools should be established, and conducted on similar principles to the metropolitan institution, and receive a proportion of its advantages, and that where such provincial schools or colleges may be established, the provincial authorities shall have prominent consideration in their control and management.

It is a remarkable fact, when the personal wealth and commercial status of English manufactures are considered, to find that the districts in which the most important branches of their operations are carried on are utterly without any fine examples available for general reference of the active capability and latent resources which the manufactures themselves possess, and of the degree of excellence to which superior skill and intelligence have already raised their productions. Great successes are occasionally heard and read of, which excite either the marvel or incredulity of those engaged in the branches of labour to which they refer; but the opportunities of seeing, studying, and appreciating such results, and, by continued examination, so thoroughly mastering the working of the processes by which their excellence has been achieved, as to be able to apply the lesson, if not with equal, at least in reference to past efforts, with improved, skill, are few and far between; while to be effectual and permanent they should be ample and continuous.

It will be deplored if, after the costly and laborious accumulation of the most valuable products of the aggregate skill and industry of the present age, resulting from the combined energies of the whole world, its exhibition should end in the excitement of a show, instead of the experience of a school becoming a transient gratification instead of a permanent advantage, and, unless some further steps be taken to render that a feeling which is now but an impulse, the ultimate benefits so trustingly looked for will, it is to be feared, be sadly curtailed.

APPENDIX B., Page 51.

Subjects which ought to be known in various Trades.

The following are answers in reply to inquiries as to the kind of instruction which ought to be given in Mechanics' Institutions to those following various trades. All the writers are men, not only of great intelligence, but of great practical experience in the various occupations to which they refer.

1. *Engineers, &c.*

The knowledge most required by them is thus stated by a Liverpool engineer:—"Mathematics, cube and square roots (to find the strength of rods and shafts); mensuration (to find the weights of machinery); practical geometry, power of levers, mechanical drawing."

In a large foundry near Manchester, one of the workmen recommends the study of the various kinds of motions, of geometry, in fact; and recommends as books, "Grier's Calculator and Dictionary," "Hibbert's Cyclopædia," "Lardner's Steam Engine," and the Mechanics' and Engineers' Magazines of London and Glasgow.

The foreman of the smiths in this foundry says, "There is but one way to make a smith, — by practice at the fire, and nothing else is required." In the same establishment I was informed "the greater part of the workmen have not received any assistance whatever from books, or from any subject of study pursued out of the shop; indeed, it is notorious that some of our most skilled workmen are, in other respects, grossly ignorant, to the extent in one or two instances of not being able to read or write, experience and practice alone supplying the necessary skill."

This statement shows forcibly how necessary Mechanics' Institutions are, even to skilful mechanics. No one denies that natural ability and manual skill are independent of school education; but the question is, will not the education greatly increase the ability and improve the skill? When so much knowledge exists bearing on the labour of mechanics, why should mechanics not acquire it?

2. *Building Trades.*

A gentleman long practically connected with the building trades makes the following statements regarding them: —

"*Joiners* ought to be able to measure their work, and give an estimate of its cost; to calculate wages, &c. This requires a knowledge of arithmetic, embracing rules up to practice and proportion, then fractions and decimals, cube and square roots. Joiners are obliged to draw out *working plans* from the architect's designs, and "set out" work. This requires practical geometry. I would recommend such a course as is given in 'Elliot's Practical Geometry and Mensuration;' and this must be regarded as merely preparatory to a more extensive course, such as contained in 'Nicholson's Guide,' which treats of roofing, &c. Most working joiners will admit that these things are *useful*, but they have yet to be convinced that these things are indispensable, and that there are others useful which they think *useless*. It is impossible to understand the principles of their work without a knowledge of theoretical geometry (Euclid). Ornamental drawing and perspective would be useful in enabling men to sketch out plans and designs of their own work. An outline of mechanics would be useful to all connected with the building trades. The mechanical powers, pressures, strength of materials, are useful to be known. These would be best learnt in class lectures, when illustrations, with appropriate apparatus, could be given.

"*Masons* require the same kind of instruction as stated for joiners.

"*Bricklayers* need less, as they work under the direction of the joiner, and they are in general satisfied with even less knowledge than they need. They ought to be able, at least, to measure their own work and make their own moulds.

"*Plasterers* should learn ornamental drawing and modelling.

"*Plumbers* should know the principles of hydrostatics and pneumatics, in addition to the arithmetic, mensuration, and practical geometry recommended for joiners."

3. *Painters.*

A house-painter in Manchester writes thus: — "In my humble opinion, a higher standard of taste must be established among those who employ house-painters, before such people as myself can have any inducements to sacrifice time and rest to acquire what at present seems unprofitable information. A great obstacle to the success of any plan for establishing a higher course of study in connection with the trade of house-painting, would be, the almost general absence of an elementary education amongst us. In such a condition, men can scarcely comprehend the aim of such plans as you would originate. There is one idea, which, if practicable, might probably establish a better order of things. If, after attending certain courses of study, working men could be furnished with a certificate or diploma — something which should be not merely honorary, but publicly recognised, and rendered almost a necessary element of success in such particular courses — then, indeed, by thus uniting knowledge and substantial advantage, there can be little doubt, despite our unfavourable social arrangements, that your project would be more successful than even you could anticipate."

4. *Factory Operatives.*

One who has "had thirty-eight years' experience of factory working, and in almost every department thereof," thus writes regarding the education necessary in this description of labour: — "For the purpose of better illustration, I will divide the factory operatives into two classes; *first*, those who only tend, or, as we name it, *tent*, the material as it passes through the various machines, from the raw cotton at the breaker or scutcher, to the cloth from the power-loom. In this class are included the scutchers, card-room hands, the piecers on the throstles and mules, and the power-loom weaver. In the *second* class are all those whose business it is to keep the various machines in good and proper working condition, and to see that those in the first class are attentive to their various duties. In this class are included the carder, the overlooker of the throstles and self-acting mules, and the power-loom jobber. It is evident that a knowledge of the construction, the connection, and dependence of every part of a machine, as well as a knowledge of the properties of the various materials of which such machine is composed, will be of the greatest advantage to the tenter, not only as preparing him for a situation as overlooker, &c. — for it is out of the most intelligent tenters that the overlookers are selected — but this knowledge will be of use to the tenter every day and in every constantly recurring circumstance in connection with his work. Those in the first class should have a knowledge of decimal fractions, of the rule of proportion, and of the extraction of the square root; and these I look upon as essential requisites to those enumerated in my second division, for without them little can be known of the calculations of the different velocities or speeds, of the draughts, or of the revolutions or twists of the threads. It may be said that such knowledge belongs more particularly to a manager; but I think all who have the hourly care of any machine ought to know all this. Besides, there are numbers of mills where no manager is kept, and where the different overlookers have the sole control in their own department. There are many books written professedly to impart the knowledge said to be necessary to the manager and overlooker, but I never yet saw one that was at all to compare with that self reliance which every manager and overlooker ought to possess, and which nothing but a perfect knowledge of the rules I have mentioned can give. A knowledge of plain trigonometry will also be of great utility ; as also a knowledge of the properties of brass, leather, oil, cotton, &c., as well as the various mechanical movements, the laws of motion, and the relative amount of friction of different metals." — *From Mr. Thomas Hogg's Circular to the Institutes of the Lancashire and Cheshire Union, 15th May,* 1850.

APPENDIX C. Page 75.

Amusements.

The cares and labours of life often leave the mind dull, and when it is relieved from them, and it must be relieved, let this be remembered, there must be seasons of relief, and the question is, how are these seasons to be filled up? When the mind enjoys relief from its occupations, I say, that relief must come in the shape of something cheering and exhilarating. The man cannot sit down dull and stupid ; and he ought not. Now, suppose that society provides him with no cheerful or attractive recreations ; that society, in fact, frowns upon all amusements ; that the importunate spirit in business, and the sanctimonious spirit in religion, and the supercilious spirit in fashion, all unite to discountenance popular sports and spectacles ; and thus, that all cheap and free enjoyments—the hale, the hearty, holiday recreations — are out of use and out of reach, what now will the man, set free from business or labour, be likely to do? He asks for relief and exhilaration; he asks for escape from his cares and anxieties ; society in its arrangements offers him none ; the tavern and the alehouse propose to supply the want, what so likely as that he will resort to the tavern and the alehouse? I have no doubt that one reason why our country fell into such unusual intemperance, was the want of simple, innocent, and authorized recreations in it. I am fully persuaded that some measure of this sort is needful, to give a natural and stable character to the temperance reform.

The reason why the French are not intemperate, is not, as is commonly thought, that their only drink is wine. They have brandy, eau de vie, and it is everywhere drank, but usually in moderation. And the reason of this is partly to be found, I believe, in their cheerfulness, in their sports and spectacles, in the resorts everywhere provided for simple entertainment.

It was remarked, during the Peninsular War, that the German soldiers, who had a variety of amusements, were never drunk on duty; while the great difficulty was to keep an English soldier from the wine house. The Germans are naturally as heavy a people as ourselves: they were once notorious for their deep potations. They are now comparatively sober. In every village are to be found music clubs. The song and the dance are frequent. But no people are more careful or industrious than the Germans.

Let it not be said, as if it were a fair reply to all this, that men are intemperate in the midst of their recreation. The question is not what they do with their vicious habits already acquired, but how they came by these habits; and the question again is not whether a man may not fall into inebriety amidst the purest recreations as well as when away from them, but what he is likely to do. In short, to do justice to the argument, it should be supposed that a people is perfectly temperate; and this may fairly be considered the question — how it is most likely to be kept so? It is certain that there is no natural appetite for spirituous drinks; but for sports and spectacles, for music and dancing, for games and theatrical representations, there is a natural inclination; and an inclination which, though often perverted, must be allowed in the original elements to be perfectly innocent, as innocent as the sportiveness of a child, or its love of beautiful colours and fine shows. But grant that the tendencies to intemperance were equally natural and strong, yet, I say, if there were among any people authorised holidays, and holiday sports; if there were evening assemblies and a pure theatre; if there were in every village a public promenade, where music might frequently be heard in the evening, would not these places be likely to draw away many from the resorts of intemperance? I confess, when I have seen of other nations tens and hundreds of thousands abroad in the public places, without any rudeness or riot among them, without one single indication of inebriety in all the crowd; when I have seen this again and again, day after day, I have asked what there is to prevent our own more intelligent people from conducting themselves with similar propriety. In seven months upon the continent of Europe, though living amidst crowds, though living in taverns, in hotels, in public houses, I have not seen four intoxicated persons. But I have seen in parks and gardens, and places of public assembly, millions of persons exhilarated by music, by spectacles, by scenery, flowers, and fragrance, cheerful without rudeness, and gay without excess.—*Rev. Orville Dewey.**

APPENDIX D. Page 79.

Exhibitions of Works of Art; Objects illustrative of general and practical Science; Specimens of Natural History; and Productions of Manufacturing Skill.

THE results of the exhibitions at Manchester and Sheffield have been so important, whether the pecuniary gain, the gratification of taste, the encouragement of a love for science, or the awakening a new appetite amongst the vast operative population of those towns be regarded, that it would be unpardonable to omit giving a few hints in this report on the manner of forming and undertaking them; observing, in the outset, that the very smallest Institution need not be discouraged by the hopelessness of rivalry with the Manchester and Sheffield Exhibitions, since the experience of the promoters of those has clearly shown that the scale of exhibition has in each instance so far exceeded the most sanguine expectations, as to warrant the belief that, in smaller towns, it is practicable to collect a valuable and interesting exhibition.

The procedure, in the collecting of the exhibitions at the towns above named (and a very similar plan has been adopted at Leeds), may be thus succinctly stated.

In the first place, the committee of the Institute has invited and secured the assistance of gentlemen of public spirit and influence, and added them to its number, to form an exhibition committee; a large committee is not desirable, being unwieldly. The next stept has been to issue a prospectus, explaining the nature, extent, and object of the exhibition, either as a circular, or as an advertisement, or both, and soliciting loans of paintings, specimens of natural history, models, &c. &c.

* See, also, Report of the Manchester and Salford Association for the better Regulation of Public Houses and other Places of Entertainment. See, also, 26th and 27th Reports (1849 and 1850) of the Chaplain to the Preston House of Correction.

The prospectus issued by the Manchester, Sheffield, and Leeds committees are each suitable documents: perhaps the first has not been excelled, and being the first, we select it as a model; it is in the form of a letter, and was largely circulated amongst the gentlemen and public bodies supposed to be favourable to the project.

"Sir,—I have the pleasure of informing you that the directors of this Institution intend, during the Christmas vacation, to open the various class and lecture-rooms for the exhibition of objects illustrative of science, art, and manufactures, and natural history; to afford the members of the Institution, and the public generally, an opportunity of inspecting, at their leisure, the present state of the arts and manufactures of the town; to bring together numerous instances of the practical application of those scientific principles so frequently expounded in our lecture-room; and thus, by blending instruction with amusement, to furnish to the great community in which we live, a source of intellectual improvement and rational recreation.

"The following outline will display the principal features of the intended exhibition, and it will, at the same time, be useful as a guide to those friends of the Institution who may be disposed to promote this object by the donation or loan of philosophical instruments, models of machinery used in the various important branches of British manufactures, and specimens illustrative of the several departments of natural history.

" *Experimental Philosophy.*

"*Statics and Dynamics.*—Instruments to illustrate the laws of equilibrium and motion of solid bodies. Elements of machinery, various kinds of levers, wheel and axle, pulleys, inclined plane, screw, and the wedge, their application to modify motion, illustrative of centrifugal force.

"*Hydrodynamics.* — Instruments to illustrate the laws of pressure, equilibrium, cohesion, and motions of fluids. Hydrostatic paradox, press, bellows, balance, &c., hydraulic machinery, water-wheels, machines driven by the reaction of water; clepsydræ, hydraulic ram; Archimides screw, blowing machines, &c.

"*Pneumatics.*— Instruments for exhibiting the mechanical properties of air and other elastic bodies; air-pumps, condensers, barometers, machines for raising water, various kinds of pumps, syphons, fire-engines, &c.

"*Heat.*—Instruments for illustrating the theory of heat: such as thermometers, pyrometers, parabolic reflectors, &c.

"*Light.*—Sectional and other models of various optical instruments: such as telescopes, microscopes, camera-obscura, camera-lucida, &c.; instruments for exhibiting the polarisation of light, optical delusion, machines for grinding lens and specula.

"*Electricity.*—Comprehending instruments for illustrating the phenomena of electricity derived from friction, galvanism, magnetism, electro-magnetism, and thermo-electricity.

"*Astronomy.*—Models of instruments for the purposes of observation and computation, such as mural circles, transit instruments, &c. Contrivances for illustrating the motions and phenomena of heavenly bodies: such as planetariums, orreries, armillary spheres, &c.

"*Geodæsy.*—Instruments in use for surveying and division of land, theodolites, levels, circumferenters, perambulators, pentographs, &c.

"*Chemistry.*—In addition to the apparatus usually employed in chemical demonstrations, it will be desirable to obtain samples of the various drugs used in the arts, particularly in the processes of bleaching, dyeing, and printing.

"*The Fine Arts.*

"*Architecture.*—Models and drawings of public buildings; specimens of materials used in their construction. Specimens of sculpture, modelling, carving, painting, engraving, &c. &c.

"*The Useful Arts.*

"*Brickwork, Masonry, and Carpentry.*—Specimens of building materials: such as stone, marble, brick, lime, cement, &c.; models of roofs, centres for bridges, specimens of various kinds of wood, &c.

"*Mill-work.*—Models to illustrate the elementary parts of mill-work, the different methods of engaging and disengaging machinery, contrivances for equalising, transmitting, and converting motion from one species to another. Models of various kinds of mills, wheels, &c.

"*Steam Engines.*—Sectional models and drawings, to exhibit the various parts of the modern steam-engine, under various forms, and their application in the single and double acting engine, high-pressure engine, vibrating engine, &c. Models for illustrating the application of steam power to mining, to navigation, to locomotive engines on railroads, and common roads.

" *Civil Engineering.*—Models and drawings of works of public and domestic utility: such as sea, river, canal, railway, and common road-works, gas-works, water-works, mining, &c.

" *Manufactures.*—Models for illustrating various manufactures from fibrous materials, with specimens in cotton, silk, flax, wool, worsted, &c.

" Models to illustrate the art of bleaching, dyeing, and calico printing.

" Models connected with the production and manufacture of cast and wrought iron and other metals.

" Models connected with the manufacture of artificial substances: as porcelain, glass, acids, salts, pigments, &c.

" Models to illustrate the arts of letter-press printing, by presses and machines; copper-plate and lithographic printing.

" *Natural History.*—Specimens of crystals, minerals, geological charts, fossils; specimens in botany; specimens in entomology, ornithology, ichthyology, zoology, &c. &c.

" By the united and zealous exertions of the members and friends of the Institution, the Directors feel assured that a source of rationable and agreeable relaxation may be established, and be made the means of diffusing a great amount of useful and interesting information.

" It will afford our ingenious mechanics and artisans a convenient opportunity of inspecting the practical application of scientific principles in the construction of machinery, of seeing the present state of perfection of our manufactures; and it is hoped it will be the means of stimulating them to scientific research, in the improvement of their respective arts, and assist them to contribute to beneficial results to this great metropolis of manufactures.

" To make this exhibition useful, attractive, and interesting, great labour will be required, as well as considerable expense. Every exertion will be made to remove the first obstacle; and with respect to the second, an appeal to our liberal townsmen, who are always willing to support works of public utility, will not be made in vain.

"To facilitate the arrangement of the Exhibition, it is very desirable that the Committee should have early information from those individuals who may be desirous of sending models and specimens to the Exhibition, and which should be delivered at the Institution not later than the second week in December, accompanied by a concise description of their character and use.

"Allow me, very respectfully, to intimate, that the Directors will be most happy to receive from you any assistance which you may be disposed to render toward the furtherance of the Exhibition; and any communication addressed to me, at the Institution, will receive immediate attention. I have the honour to be, Sir, your most obedient servant,

"SAMUEL E. COLTANN, Sec.

"17, Cooper Street, Manchester, Nov. 1837."

This circular will give a good general idea of the scope of these Exhibitions. The details of management are of considerable importance. At Leeds, the General Committee was subdivided into four; viz.,—a Committee for collecting philosophical apparatus;—a Committee for collecting specimens of the Fine Arts;—a Committee for collecting models of machinery, and specimens of manufacture;—and a Committee for collecting specimens of Natural History. Each of these reported from time to time to the General Committee, so as to secure unity of operation. Promises of loans are recorded in proper minute books, and in due time an Arrangement Committee is formed to receive or collect the loans, to place them in suitable situations in the Exhibition rooms, number them, and prepare the catalogue. The duties of this Committee are exceedingly important, as on it depends, not only the proper arrangement and classification of the specimens, but the keeping of a correct account of them when received, so as to facilitate the safe and proper return to the owners at the close of the Exhibition. The plan adopted at Sheffield appears to be at once simple and efficient, viz.,—to appoint a porter to receive and record all specimens, and to place on each a number corresponding to a consecutive series in the receiving book. This book has a column for the insertion of the catalogue number, thereby admitting of easy reference from one to the other; if the catalogue had also a column for the porter's number, the two would be completed. At the end of the porter's book is an index of the names of the lenders, and the number of the specimens belonging to them.

So soon as specimens begin to arrive — and the time must be determined by the General Committee — two or more members of the Committee are always in attendance at the rooms, and the same plan is adopted throughout the whole period of the Exhibition. The property is fully insured, for the safety alike of the Committee and lenders, the former being of course pledged to make good all loss or damage.

A low charge for admission is necessary to success, it being found that the lower the charge the greater the resort; or, in other words, that numbers, and not the price of admission, determine the amount of receipts.

The introduction of some one or more curious and interesting manufacturing engines or implements, such as a silk loom at work; or a small steam-engine working a model machine of any kind; or an oxyhydrogen microscope; a fountain in full play; a small lake or reservoir, with a steam-packet plying round it; a glass-blower, forming curious glass toys; a printing or lithographic press; an electrical machine, occasionally at work, &c., &c., has been found to be exceedingly attractive; and it may be worth the consideration of the Committee whether, when the Exhibition is open in the summer months, a small botanical collection might not be added.— *From the Yorkshire Union Report for* 1839.

APPENDIX E., Page 131.

Itinerating Libraries for Villages.

There are numerous places containing small populations, where the inclination or the means, or possibly both, are wanting to organize an Institution. The obstacles are various: such as the leading inhabitants entertaining a prejudice against snch institutes; the want of a sufficient number of persons to form a good working committee; the absence of a suitable building for the purposes of the institute; and various other causes might be enumerated. Very often it will be found that the advantages which such an institution is calculated to afford, are not appreciated, simply because they have not been enjoyed. Ignorance is not only a cause, but an effect; and if we could but once put the treasures of knowledge within the reach of many of the working-classes, they would be glad to provide them afterwards for themselves. Too far from the large towns to avail themselves of the help of our larger institutions, and too few in numbers to organize an useful institution for themselves, the inhabitants of many of our small villages must either be assisted by some such association as the Yorkshire Union, or they must be altogether shut out from the beneficial influences which larger places can command.

Nine villages in Cumberland are united under the title of the "United Villages Perambulating Library." It consists of nearly 300 volumes, and has 400 members, each paying one penny per month. The books are deposited at nine stations, one in each village, under the care of a suitable person; every six weeks a paid messenger removes the books in boxes provided for that purpose. All the stations are on a footing of perfect equality as to priority in receiving the fresh books. At first it was principally intended to benefit the younger portion of the community, but its success slightly changed this feature.

From the Parliamentary Report on Public Libraries[85], it appears that the plan of itinerating libraries has prevailed extensively in Scotland. It was introduced into the Highlands by the General Assembly of the Church of Scotland, and into Peeblesshire by the Free Church, owing to the success which had attended it in East Lothian, where the plan has been in operation twenty-five years. It was originated by Mr. Samuel Brown, of Haddington. In the latter district there was, at one time, as many as fifty stations, at each of which 50 volumes were deposited. The whole of the books were issued, on an average, five times in the course of a year. Some of the books were issued eighteen times, and some as many as thirty times in two years. Very often there was not a single book to be found in the libraries. The evidence as to the benefits conferred by it was very favourable, and the writers stated that the first Mechanics' Institution at Haddington and Dunbar originated out of the interest excited by those libraries. The books were changed only every two years. And one proof of the great importance of the tolerably frequent change of books in such libraries is offered in the fact, that the circulation always fell off in the second year, generally in the proportion of one-third,

[85] Evidence of Rev. John Croumbie Brown, page 3.

and rose again with the introduction of new books. Shopkeepers and schoolmasters were found to make the most effective librarians, from the facilities they possessed of giving out the books. It was also stated, that the success of the plan mainly depended on the securing of zealous librarians. As the librarians must have been the parties generally best cognizant of the utility of their labours, it is strongly confirmative of the advantages, that no difficulty was found in securing a sufficient number of persons willing to undertake the task without any remuneration, and simply as a means of doing good. Much of the original success of the undertaking seems to have been attributable to the energy of the founder of the plan, the father of the witness. With the withdrawal of his help, the library declined. Another cause is to be found in the fact, that no charge was made for the books for the space of fourteen or fifteen years, and those who had the books gratuitously, would, as is usual, consider it a hardship to be called upon to pay. The plan, however, is still in successful working in about twenty divisions in the western district of East Lothian; and the witness, after his long and extensive experience in connection with its practical working, is as confident as ever of the good results of the plan, and the practicability of a much greater extension of it. The same plan has been tried on a small scale in connexion with the Northern Union of Mechanics' Institutes. The secretary, Mr. J. L. Thornton, says of it: — "With respect to the itinerating library in conjunction with the Union, it has already surpassed the most sanguine expectations its projectors anticipated; and, if adequately supported, bids fair to become one of the most efficient mediums hitherto devised among unions for the dissemination of knowledge. In rural situations particularly, where the supply of new books is necessarily limited and soon exhausted, the advantages this scheme affords are sought with extreme avidity. So great, indeed, has the demand become, that the number of works is insufficient to supply each society with complete sets. The Committee, therefore, after an experience of two years, have matured the practical working of their project, and strengthened their conviction of the benefits it is calculated to diffuse. During the year, seven societies in the Union have availed themselves of the advantages of the library, with much benefit, there can be little doubt, to the bulk of the members."[86]

[86] Third Report of Northern Union of Mechanics' Institutes.

Who can calculate the amount of good which such an agency will effect? Who can say how many, previously shut out from books, — the greatest of civilizers, — may now, by this simple and inexpensive machinery, form tastes and acquire habits of the greatest importance to their welfare in life? Speaking on the subject of Lending Libraries, the North British Review observes, "Everybody who lends a good book to a person unable to obtain the use of books from other sources, does a great thing. To establish a lending library in a village, no matter how small, is proportionately a greater thing. * * * An isolated lending library in a country village is a very good thing; but it requires the support of other lending libraries in the neighbourhood to render it permanently efficacious. On its first establishment, there is sure to be a heavy run upon it. The novelty of having books at command is something exhilarating and exciting; and the villagers, especially the boys and the girls, and the old people who are past work, are continually coming to exchange them. But, after a while, the demand begins to languish. The readers have 'had the pick' of the library, and they either have, or think they have, had all the books that they care to read. If, then, the proprietor of the library can, at this point, exchange it for another established in a neighbouring village, he can revive the declining appetite by offering his neighbours a feast of new intellectual food. There will be again a run upon the book shelves, and again pleasant and improving occupation will be in the reach of all who have their own time at their disposal, and who are often driven into evil courses, solely by the want of 'something better to do.'" [87]

The advantages of such a plan, besides those already mentioned, would be: —

1st. The library might be rendered almost, probably entirely, self-supporting, after the expense of its first establishing had been defrayed.

2nd. The selection of books, being in the Committee of the Union (all gentlemen practically familiar with the task of selecting works for Mechanics' Institutes), would be such as to insure their suitableness for the objects contemplated.

3rd. No public agitation, such as is needful for the establishment of an institute, would be required; one competent

[87] Review, No. 33, page 97.

person in a village willing to take charge of such a library would be sufficient.

4th. The establishment of a library would be likely to attract additional help from local sources. In some cases it might lead to the formation of classes, and the other departments of a Mechanics' Institute. — *Extract from a Letter addressed to the Leeds' Mercury by the Secretary of the Yorkshire Union of Mechanics' Institutes.*

APPENDIX F., Page 155.

Museums.

A certain stock of specimens is necessary (as a general apparatus) for public instruction; but this is soon acquired: the great mass of our museums look much beyond this; they seek specimens from abroad, as much for display as use, at great cost and labour. Yet it is precisely what is nearest at hand and cheapest, that, after all, is the most valuable. On no objects are the faculties so likely to be well exercised as on objects within every-day reach; the results of inquiry are sure to be more accurate, subject as they are to much stricter and frequent tests; they lead to more immediate utility; they are the very materials of all after knowledge; they are more or less interwoven with all the purposes of local life. The formation of a local museum, carried on by the institution according to the peculiar dispositions and opportunities of its members, necessarily leads to all this. Whilst one party or individual is engaged with local mineralogy or geology, another with local natural history, a third with local antiquities, a fourth is occupied with local statistics and economics, and all more or less pass through a course, of all others, to themselves and their districts the most beneficial,— a course of thorough study of those matters in which, one way or other, they are for the rest of their life most likely to be engaged.

In the meantime the collection proceeds without drawing on their purse; the materials are found in their daily walk. But it must not on that account be considered less precious to others as well as themselves. Where communication is so easy, and science ready to avail itself, at the earliest notice, of every discovery, the more complete these local museums the quicker must be the general progress of all science. What the traveller looks for on arriving at a town is, not what he has left behind him in another, not indifferent duplicates of the great collections of the larger towns; but what is special to the town, however small, and to the district itself. No one can enter the museums and model galleries of Italy, France, Belgium, Germany, &c. &c., without being struck by the extensive and important additions made by this local spirit, working on its special territory, to the general treasures. Archæology profits by it in Italy. It sets the excavator to work in every field, on every hillock, and has thus done more to detect the ancient world of their forefathers than the purses of princes. — *On the Lyceum System in America, by J. Wyse, Esq. M.P., page* 212, *in 2nd Publication of the Central Society of Education.*

THE END.

INDEX

For Product Safety Concerns and Information please contact our EU representative GPSR@taylorandfrancis.com
Taylor & Francis Verlag GmbH, Kaufingerstraße 24, 80331 München, Germany

www.ingramcontent.com/pod-product-compliance
Lightning Source LLC
LaVergne TN
LVHW011132300926
849160LV00008B/617

* 9 7 8 1 1 3 8 9 9 3 5 1 8 *